ECOLOGY
Earth's Natural Resources

Anthea Maton
Former NSTA National Coordinator
Project Scope, Sequence, Coordination
Washington, DC

Jean Hopkins
Science Instructor and Department Chairperson
John H. Wood Middle School
San Antonio, Texas

Susan Johnson
Professor of Biology
Ball State University
Muncie, Indiana

David LaHart
Senior Instructor
Florida Solar Energy Center
Cape Canaveral, Florida

Charles William McLaughlin
Science Instructor and Department Chairperson
Central High School
St. Joseph, Missouri

Maryanna Quon Warner
Science Instructor
Del Dios Middle School
Escondido, California

Jill D. Wright
Professor of Science Education
Director of International Field Programs
University of Pittsburgh
Pittsburgh, Pennsylvania

Prentice Hall
Englewood Cliffs, New Jersey
Needham, Massachusetts

Prentice Hall Science

Ecology: Earth's Natural Resources

Student Text and Annotated Teacher's Edition
Laboratory Manual
Teacher's Resource Package
Teacher's Desk Reference
Computer Test Bank
Teaching Transparencies
Science Reader
Product Testing Activities
Computer Courseware
Video and Interactive Video

The illustration on the cover, rendered by Joseph Cellini, depicts the results of pollution on one of the Earth's most precious natural resources—a pristine stream.

Credits begin on page 129.

FIRST EDITION

ISBN 0-13-987082-2

4 5 6 7 8 9 10   96 95 94 93

Prentice Hall
A Division of Simon & Schuster
Englewood Cliffs, New Jersey 07632

STAFF CREDITS

Editorial:	Harry Bakalian, Pamela E. Hirschfeld, Maureen Grassi, Robert P. Letendre, Elisa Mui Eiger, Lorraine Smith-Phelan, Christine A. Caputo
Design:	AnnMarie Roselli, Carmela Pereira, Susan Walrath, Leslie Osher, Art Soares
Production:	Suse Cioffi, Joan McCulley, Elizabeth Torjussen, Christina Burghard, Marlys Lehmann
Photo Research:	Libby Forsyth, Emily Rose, Martha Conway
Publishing Technology:	Andrew Grey Bommarito, Gwendollynn Waldron, Deborah Jones, Monduane Harris, Michael Colucci, Gregory Myers, Cleasta Wilburn
Marketing:	Andy Socha, Victoria Willows
Pre-Press Production:	Laura Sanderson, Denise Herckenrath
Manufacturing:	Rhett Conklin, Gertrude Szyferblatt

Consultants

Kathy French	National Science Consultant
William Royalty	National Science Consultant

Contributing Writers

Linda Densman
Science Instructor
Hurst, TX

Linda Grant
Former Science Instructor
Weatherford, TX

Heather Hirschfeld
Science Writer
Durham, NC

Marcia Mungenast
Science Writer
Upper Montclair, NJ

Michael Ross
Science Writer
New York City, NY

Content Reviewers

Dan Anthony
Science Mentor
Rialto, CA

John Barrow
Science Instructor
Pomona, CA

Leslie Bettencourt
Science Instructor
Harrisville, RI

Carol Bishop
Science Instructor
Palm Desert, CA

Dan Bohan
Science Instructor
Palm Desert, CA

Steve M. Carlson
Science Instructor
Milwaukie, OR

Larry Flammer
Science Instructor
San Jose, CA

Steve Ferguson
Science Instructor
Lee's Summit, MO

Robin Lee Harris Freedman
Science Instructor
Fort Bragg, CA

Edith H. Gladden
Former Science Instructor
Philadelphia, PA

Vernita Marie Graves
Science Instructor
Tenafly, NJ

Jack Grube
Science Instructor
San Jose, CA

Emiel Hamberlin
Science Instructor
Chicago, IL

Dwight Kertzman
Science Instructor
Tulsa, OK

Judy Kirschbaum
Science/Computer Instructor
Tenafly, NJ

Kenneth L. Krause
Science Instructor
Milwaukie, OR

Ernest W. Kuehl, Jr.
Science Instructor
Bayside, NY

Mary Grace Lopez
Science Instructor
Corpus Christi, TX

Warren Maggard
Science Instructor
PeWee Valley, KY

Della M. McCaughan
Science Instructor
Biloxi, MS

Stanley J. Mulak
Former Science Instructor
Jensen Beach, FL

Richard Myers
Science Instructor
Portland, OR

Carol Nathanson
Science Mentor
Riverside, CA

Sylvia Neivert
Former Science Instructor
San Diego, CA

Jarvis VNC Pahl
Science Instructor
Rialto, CA

Arlene Sackman
Science Instructor
Tulare, CA

Christine Schumacher
Science Instructor
Pikesville, MD

Suzanne Steinke
Science Instructor
Towson, MD

Len Svinth
*Science Instructor/
Chairperson*
Petaluma, CA

Elaine M. Tadros
Science Instructor
Palm Desert, CA

Joyce K. Walsh
Science Instructor
Midlothian, VA

Steve Weinberg
Science Instructor
West Hartford, CT

Charlene West, PhD
Director of Curriculum
Rialto, CA

John Westwater
Science Instructor
Medford, MA

Glenna Wilkoff
Science Instructor
Chesterfield, OH

Edee Norman Wiziecki
Science Instructor
Urbana, IL

Teacher Advisory Panel

Beverly Brown
Science Instructor
Livonia, MI

James Burg
Science Instructor
Cincinnati, OH

Karen M. Cannon
Science Instructor
San Diego, CA

John Eby
Science Instructor
Richmond, CA

Elsie M. Jones
Science Instructor
Marietta, GA

Michael Pierre McKereghan
Science Instructor
Denver, CO

Donald C. Pace, Sr.
Science Instructor
Reisterstown, MD

Carlos Francisco Sainz
Science Instructor
National City, CA

William Reed
Science Instructor
Indianapolis, IN

Multicultural Consultant

Steven J. Rakow
Associate Professor
*University of Houston—
Clear Lake*
Houston, TX

English as a Second Language (ESL) Consultants

Jaime Morales
Bilingual Coordinator
Huntington Park, CA

Pat Hollis Smith
Former ESL Instructor
Beaumont, TX

Reading Consultant

Larry Swinburne
Director
*Swinburne Readability
Laboratory*

CONTENTS

ECOLOGY: EARTH'S NATURAL RESOURCES

Reference Section

Features

CONCEPT MAPPING

T hroughout your study of science, you will learn a variety of terms, facts, figures, and concepts. Each new topic you encounter will provide its own collection of words and ideas—which, at times, you may think seem endless. But each of the ideas within a particular topic is related in some way to the others. No concept in science is isolated. Thus it will help you to understand the topic if you see the whole picture; that is, the interconnectedness of all the individual terms and ideas. This is a much more effective and satisfying way of learning than memorizing separate facts.

Actually, this should be a rather familiar process for you. Although you may not think about it in this way, you analyze many of the elements in your daily life by looking for relationships or connections. For example, when you look at a collection of flowers, you may divide them into groups: roses, carnations, and daisies. You may then associate colors with these flowers: red, pink, and white. The general topic is flowers. The subtopic is types of flowers. And the colors are specific terms that describe flowers. A topic makes more sense and is more easily understood if you understand how it is broken down into individual ideas and how these ideas are related to one another and to the entire topic.

It is often helpful to organize information visually so that you can see how it all fits together. One technique for describing related ideas is called a **concept map**. In a concept map, an idea is represented by a word or phrase enclosed in a box. There are several ideas in any concept map. A connection between two ideas is made with a line. A word or two that describes the connection is written on or near the line. The general topic is located at the top of the map. That topic is then broken down into subtopics, or more specific ideas, by branching lines. The most specific topics are located at the bottom of the map.

To construct a concept map, first identify the important ideas or key terms in the chapter or section. Do not try to include too much information. Use your judgment as to what is really important. Write the general topic at the top of your map. Let's use an example to help illustrate this process. Suppose you decide that the key terms in a section you are reading are School, Living Things, Language Arts, Subtraction, Grammar, Mathematics, Experiments, Papers, Science, Addition, Novels. The general topic is School. Write and enclose this word in a box at the top of your map.

SCHOOL

Now choose the subtopics—Language Arts, Science, Mathematics. Figure out how they are related to the topic. Add these words to your map. Continue this procedure until you have included all the important ideas and terms. Then use lines to make the appropriate connections between ideas and terms. Don't forget to write a word or two on or near the connecting line to describe the nature of the connection.

Do not be concerned if you have to redraw your map (perhaps several times!) before you show all the important connections clearly. If, for example, you write papers for Science as well as for Language Arts, you may want to place these two subjects next to each other so that the lines do not overlap.

One more thing you should know about concept mapping: Concepts can be correctly mapped in many different ways. In fact, it is unlikely that any two people will draw identical concept maps for a complex topic. Thus there is no one correct concept map for any topic! Even though your concept map may not match those of your classmates, it will be correct as long as it shows the most important concepts and the clear relationships among them. Your concept map will also be correct if it has meaning to you and if it helps you understand the material you are reading. A concept map should be so clear that if some of the terms are erased, the missing terms could easily be filled in by following the logic of the concept map.

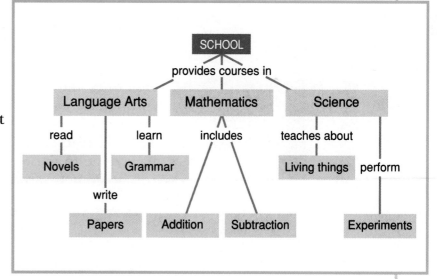

ECOLOGY

Earth's Natural Resources

Is there a solar-powered telephone in your future? As nonrenewable energy resources are used up, solar energy and other alternative sources of energy will become increasingly important.

Like the United States, most countries rely on coal and oil, mined or drilled from the Earth, to produce the energy they need. But Iceland, a small island nation in the North Atlantic, mines "volcanic fires." Iceland sits atop a chain of volcanoes covering one third of its territory. Heat generated within the Earth, or geothermal energy, provides Iceland with energy for home heating, electricity, and manufacturing.

Iceland's use of geothermal energy demonstrates how clean, inexpensive alternative energy sources can be used to meet people's energy needs. As you read the chapters that follow, you will learn about various energy resources and their importance for present and future use. You will also learn about Earth's other nonliving resources: land, water, and air. You will read about the damage that people have done to these resources and find out what can be done to protect them.

An off-shore oil-drilling platform lights up the ocean at dusk. But obtaining and using energy resources such as oil can be harmful to the environment.

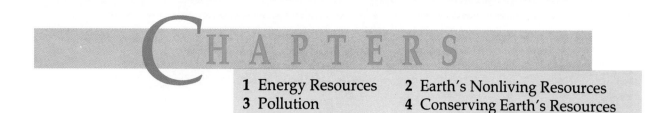

CHAPTERS

▲ *How can we save the Earth from polluted air and water? The use of wind generators and widespread recycling can help.*

Discovery *Activity*

Reusable Paper

1. Soak some shredded newspaper in warm water overnight.

2. Mash the soaked newspaper into a pulpy mixture.

3. Cover your work area with a sheet of waxed paper. Spread a thin layer of the pulpy mixture on the waxed paper.

4. Cover the mixture with plastic wrap. Let the mixture dry overnight. What does the dried mixture look and feel like?

   ■ What could you use your reusable paper mixture for?

   ■ Why is reusing paper a good idea?

Energy Resources

Guide for Reading

After you read the following sections, you will be able to

1–1 What Are Fossil Fuels?

■ Describe three main types of fossil fuels and their uses.

1–2 Energy From the Sun

■ Compare active and passive solar heating.

1–3 Wind and Water

■ Discuss the use of wind generators and hydroelectric power.

1–4 Nuclear Energy

■ Compare nuclear fission and nuclear fusion.

■ Describe the parts of a nuclear reactor.

1–5 Alternative Energy Sources

■ Discuss the nature and importance of alternative energy sources.

What is 221 meters high, 379 meters long, 14 meters thick at the top, 201 meters thick at the bottom, and contains 2.5 million cubic meters of concrete? Give up? The answer is the Hoover Dam, the highest concrete dam in the Western Hemisphere. This huge dam is located in a canyon on the Colorado River between Nevada and Arizona.

You may wonder why enormous amounts of time and money were spent to build this mammoth structure. One reason for the effort was to control the flow of the Colorado River and provide irrigation for surrounding farmlands. The other equally important reason was to generate hydroelectric power. Hoover Dam's 17 electric generators provide electricity for 500,000 homes in Nevada, Arizona, and California.

Hydroelectric power—electricity generated by water—currently provides 13.5 percent of all the electricity produced in the United States. Where does the rest of our electricity come from? What are some other sources of energy for today and tomorrow? You will find the answers to these questions in the pages that follow.

Journal *Activity*

You and Your World What do you think your life might have been like 100 years ago, before the widespread use of electricity? How would it have been different from your life today? In your journal, describe what a typical day without electricity might be like.

This aerial view of Hoover Dam in Nevada shows the dam and the power plant in the foreground and Lake Mead in the background.

Guide for Reading

Focus on these questions as you read.

- *What are the three main fossil fuels?*
- *What are some uses of fossil fuels?*

1–1 What Are Fossil Fuels?

Stop for a minute and think about the many ways in which you use energy every day. Pretty impressive list, isn't it? Where does all this energy come from? More than 90 percent of the energy used in the United States—energy to light and heat your home and to run the family car—comes from **fossil fuels.** Fossil fuels formed hundreds of millions of years ago from the remains of dead plants and animals. The dead plants and animals were buried under layers of sediments such as mud, sand, silt, and clay. Over millions of years, heat and pressure changed the sediments into rocks and the plant and animal remains into fossil fuels. **The three main fossil fuels are coal, oil, and natural gas.**

Why are fossil fuels so useful as energy sources? The answer has to do with their chemical makeup. Fossil fuels are rich in **hydrocarbons.** Hydrocarbons are substances that contain the elements hydrogen and carbon (thus their name). The chart in Figure 1–1 lists some simple hydrocarbons.

Figure 1–1 *This chart lists some simple hydrocarbons and their chemical formulas. What is the name of the hydrocarbon used for bottled gas? What is its formula?*

SOME SIMPLE HYDROCARBONS

Name	Chemical Formula	Use
Methane	CH_4	Major part of natural gas; raw material for many synthetic products
Ethane	C_2H_6	Used to make ethyl alcohol, acetic acid, and other chemicals; refrigerant
Propane	C_3H_8	"Bottled gas" for home heating, portable stoves and heaters; refrigerant
Butane	C_4H_{10}	Used in portable lighters, home heating fuel, portable stoves and heaters
Pentane	C_5H_{12}	Solvent; measuring column in low-temperature thermometers
Hexane	C_6H_{14}	Major component of materials used in certain motor fuels and dry-cleaning solvents
Heptane	C_7H_{16}	Main part of turpentine from Jeffrey pine
Octane	C_8H_{18}	Important part of gasoline fuel for cars, trucks, buses, and the like

When the hydrocarbons in fossil fuels are combined with oxygen at high temperatures, heat energy and light energy are released. This process, commonly called burning, is known as **combustion.**

Other types of fuels also give off heat and light during the process of combustion. For example, people have been burning wood as a fuel ever since early cave dwellers learned how to start a fire. But wood does not produce as much energy per kilogram as fossil fuels do. One kilogram of coal, for example, provides twice as much heat as one kilogram of wood. The amount of heat energy provided by oil and natural gas is more than three times that provided by wood. In addition, fossil fuels are easier to transport, store, and use than wood is.

Despite these advantages, the use of fossil fuels presents several problems. Some deposits of coal and oil contain large amounts of sulfur. When these high-sulfur fuels are burned, they release dangerous pollutants such as sulfur dioxide into the atmosphere. You will learn more about the problem of pollution caused by the burning of fossil fuels in Chapter 3.

FIND OUT BY READING

Life in the Coal Mines

Coal mining has traditionally been hard and dangerous work—not exactly the stuff of poetry. But for a look at the life of a coal miner from a poet's point of view, you might want to read the poem *Calaban in the Coal Mines* by the American poet and critic Louis Untermeyer (1885–1977).

Coal

Coal is a solid fossil fuel. Historical records show that coal has been used in Europe for at least 4000 years. And Native Americans were using coal 400 years before Christopher Columbus was born! There are four types of coal, each of which represents a different stage of development. Each type of coal can be used as a fuel.

The first type of coal is **peat.** (Actually, peat is not really coal but only the first stage in the development of coal.) Peat is a soft substance made of decayed plant fibers. When burned, it gives off a great deal of smoke but little heat energy.

Pressure from the layers of rock above it changes peat into **lignite** (LIHG-night), the second type of coal. Lignite, or brown coal, is soft and has a woody texture. It is also low in heat energy.

Added pressure turns lignite into **bituminous** (bigh-TOO-muh-nuhs) **coal,** the third type of coal. Bituminous coal, which is dark brown or black, is also called soft coal. It is found deep within the

Figure 1–2 *The four types of coal are shown in this photograph. Going counterclockwise from the top right, they are peat, lignite, bituminous, and anthracite. Which is the hardest type of coal?*

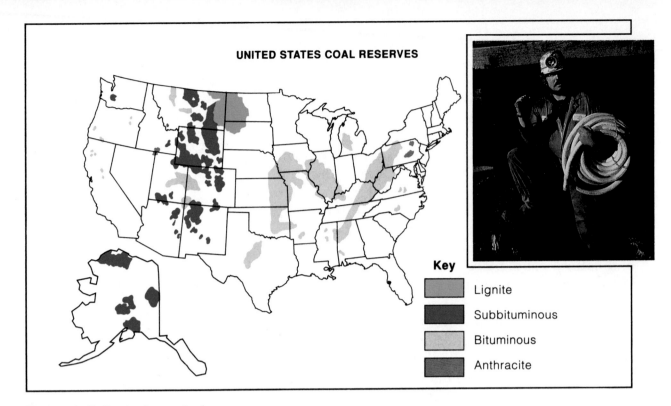

UNITED STATES COAL RESERVES

Key
- Lignite
- Subbituminous
- Bituminous
- Anthracite

Figure 1–3 *Coal miners dig for coal in deep underground mine shafts. Major coal reserves are located throughout the United States. Where is the coal deposit nearest your home located?*

Earth. Bituminous coal is the most abundant type of coal.

Tremendous pressure causes bituminous coal to change into **anthracite** (AN-thruh-sight), the fourth type of coal. Anthracite, or hard coal, is extremely hard and brittle. It is almost pure carbon. The map in Figure 1–3 shows the major coal reserves in the United States. Reserves are known deposits that can be developed economically using current technology. According to the map in Figure 1–3, where are the only reserves of anthracite located in the United States?

Oil and Natural Gas

Liquid fossil fuel is called oil, or petroleum. Oil is found in areas that were once covered by oceans. When plants and animals in the oceans died, they sank to the ocean floor and were covered by sediments. In time, the layers of sediments changed into rocks such as limestone, sandstone, and shale. Pressure from these rock layers, as well as great heat and the action of certain bacteria, changed the plant and animal remains into oil.

Limestone and sandstone contain tiny pores, or openings. Oil droplets probably seeped through

these pores and through cracks in the rock layers, forming underground pools of oil. Oil that is removed from these underground deposits is called crude oil.

Almost all the crude oil used in the world today is obtained by drilling wells into underground deposits. Some oil, however, is located near the surface of the Earth. Two sources of oil located near the Earth's surface are tar sands and oil shale. Tar sands are layers of sand soaked with thick, gooey petroleum. Oil shale is a gray rock containing a tarlike material. When oil shale is heated to a high temperature (about 600°C), it releases a hydrocarbon vapor that can be condensed (changed from the gas phase to the liquid phase) into crude oil. Unfortunately, obtaining oil from tar sands and oil shale is difficult and, therefore, not economical.

The third type of fossil fuel is natural gas. Natural gas is usually found associated with oil deposits. Because natural gas is less dense than oil, it rises above the oil. As a result, natural gas deposits are usually located above oil deposits. See Figure 1–5. The most common natural gas is methane.

Figure 1-4 *To obtain crude oil, wells may be drilled beneath the ocean floor. Oil from deposits in Alaska is transported through the Alaska pipeline. Oil shale may contain enough oil to be ignited.*

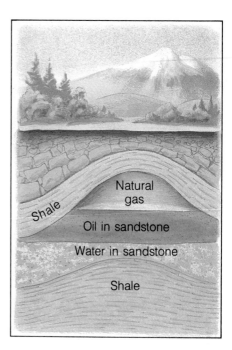

Figure 1-5 *Oil and natural gas are often found in the same deposit. Why is the natural gas usually found above the oil?*

FIND OUT BY DOING

Where Is the Oil?

Using books and other reference materials in your school library or the public library, find out where the major oil deposits in the world are located. Make a map showing the locations of these oil deposits. If possible, differentiate among areas of reserves that are currently producing oil, areas of recently discovered deposits, and areas that are believed to contain oil.

Uses of Fossil Fuels

Fossil fuels—coal, oil, and natural gas—are the main sources of energy for industry, transportation, and homes. Industry is the major consumer of fossil fuels, closely followed by transportation. The charts in Figure 1–6 illustrate the major uses of oil and coal in the United States. Most of the coal produced in the United States is used to generate electricity. Transportation relies on liquid fuels, such as gasoline, that are produced from crude oil.

Crude oil is used to make many of the products you use every day. The crude oil brought up from beneath the Earth's surface is a mixture of many hydrocarbons in addition to certain impurities. Before the crude oil can be used, it must be refined. That is, the impurities must be removed. Then the oil is used to make heating oil for homes, gasoline for automobiles, kerosene for lamps, waxes for candles, asphalt for roads, and **petrochemicals.** Petrochemicals are useful substances that are derived from oil or natural gas. Some petrochemicals are used to make plastics, fabrics, medicines, and building materials. Can you name some other petrochemical products?

Natural gas is a popular source of energy for home heating because it is less expensive and cleaner to use than oil or coal. Limited reserves, however, may cut down on the use of natural gas in the future.

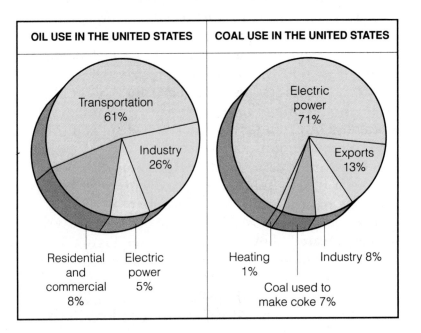

Figure 1–6 These charts show the various uses of oil and coal in the United States. What percentage of the oil is used for transportation? What is most of the coal used for?

Figure 1-7 *A wide variety of products, such as plastics, can be derived from crude oil after it is refined. What are useful products derived from oil or natural gas called?*

Fossil Fuel Shortages

Since 1900, the population of the United States has increased from 76 million people to more than 250 million at the time of the most recent census in 1990. During the same period, energy use in the United States has increased 10 times. In fact, the United States, with only 5 percent of the world's population, now uses more than 30 percent of all the energy produced in the world today!

The reserves of fossil fuels in the Earth are limited. In fact, scientists estimate that in a relatively brief period in the Earth's history (less than 500 years), we will have used up almost all the coal, oil, and natural gas formed over a period of 500 million years! In only one day, humans use an amount of oil that took about 1000 years to form. At the present rate of use, the United States may run out of fossil fuels by the year 2060. By the year 2080, the entire world may run out of fossil fuels. How do you think the absence of fossil fuels will affect living conditions in the United States? Worldwide?

In the United States, coal is more abundant than oil and natural gas. Today, coal supplies about 20 percent of the energy used in this country. At the present rate of use, coal reserves may last another

Figure 1–8 *Coal is the most abundant fossil fuel present in the United States. What will eventually happen to these coal reserves?*

300 years. But more coal is used for energy production—chiefly electricity—every year. Coal may become the main fossil fuel resource by the year 2000. In that case, reserves of coal will run out much sooner than originally estimated. It is important to remember, however, that mining and burning coal is harmful to the environment. You will learn more about the problems associated with the production and use of coal in Chapter 3.

Geologists are hard at work trying to find new sources of fossil fuels. Alternative energy sources are also being developed. Some of these alternative sources are discussed in the sections that follow. But conservation of current fossil fuel resources is still the best way to provide energy for the future. A thorough discussion of the need for conservation of energy resources is included in Chapter 4. Think about ways of conserving energy as you read the sections that follow and as you go about your daily routine. For example, what ways can you think of to conserve fossil fuels?

CAREERS

Geophysical Prospector

Oil deposits exist beneath every ocean and continent. But before oil can be recovered, it must be located. Scientists who locate oil reserves are **geophysical prospectors.** They study rock formations from which they prepare maps. The maps are then used to determine drilling spots.

To learn more about a career as a geophysical prospector, write to the Society of Exploration Geo-Physicists, PO Box 702740, Tulsa, OK 74101.

1–1 Section Review

1. Identify the three main types of fossil fuels.
2. What are the major uses of fossil fuels in the United States?
3. What are the four types of coal? Which represents the first stage in the development of coal? The last?
4. What are petrochemicals? List three products that are derived from petrochemicals.

Critical Thinking—*Making Inferences*
5. Oil and natural gas deposits were formed from the remains of plants and animals that lived in the oceans millions of years ago. Today, however, many oil and natural gas wells are located on dry land. Suggest an explanation for this fact.

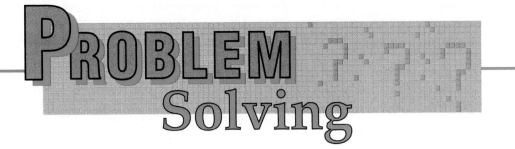

Solving

Examining World Oil Production

The graph below illustrates the world's crude oil production for the years 1900 to 1990. The dotted lines represent a prediction of crude oil production from 1990 to 2100. Use the graph to answer the questions that follow. (OPEC stands for the Organization of Petroleum Exporting Countries. The OPEC countries are Algeria, Ecuador, Gabon, Indonesia, Iran, Iraq, Kuwait, Libya, Nigeria, Quatar, Saudi Arabia, United Arab Emirates, and Venezuela.)

1. When was the production of crude oil in the United States at its peak?

2. According to the prediction, when will the United States stop producing crude oil?

3. What was the largest amount of crude oil produced in the world in a single year?

4. According to the prediction, what is the total amount of crude oil that will be produced by all countries in the year 2100?

5. Making Predictions According to the prediction, most of the crude oil reserves in the United States will be exhausted early in the next century. What sources of energy do you think we may be using for heating, cooling, transportation, and electricity in 2050?

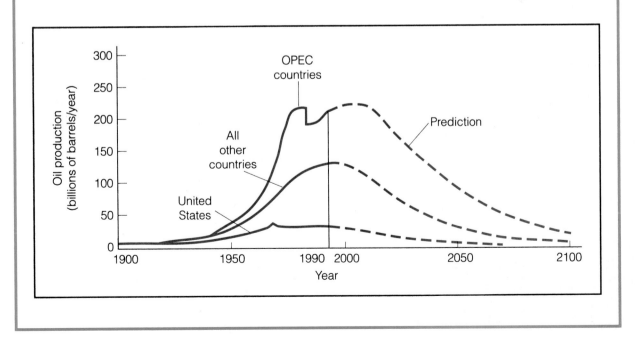

1–2 Energy From the Sun

Life on Earth would not be possible without energy from the sun, or **solar energy.** Without solar energy, plants would not grow, rain would not fall, and winds would not blow. Earth would be a cold, dark planet on which nothing could survive.

Scientists estimate that the solar energy received by the Earth in one day is enough to meet the world's energy needs for 30 years at the present rate of energy use. **Solar energy can be used to heat buildings and to produce electricity.** To be useful, however, solar energy must first be collected, converted, and stored. Why are collection, conversion, and storage necessary?

Solar energy is spread out over a wide area, not concentrated in one place. So solar energy must be collected before it can be used. In addition, most of the sun's energy is received in the form of light. Thus, sunlight must be converted into other forms of energy, such as heat and electricity, before it can be used. And finally, solar energy must be stored for use when the sun is not shining (at night or during cloudy weather). There are several ways to solve the problems of collection, conversion, and storage of solar energy. Solar-heating systems for homes, schools, and commercial buildings may be one answer.

Passive Solar Heating

Solar-heating systems can be either passive or active. In a passive solar-heating system, the windows of a building are positioned so that sunlight enters directly and heats the building. Shades covering the windows hold in the heat during the night. An overhang prevents too much heat from entering during the summer.

The obvious problem with passive solar heating is that when the sun is not shining, the source of heat is removed. To solve this problem, a backup heating system is needed. In a passive solar home, a small wood stove can often be used as the backup system.

Passive solar heating can also be used to heat water for home use, such as for bathing, showering,

Figure 1–9 *Without energy from the sun, life on Earth would not be possible. What is another name for energy from the sun?*

Figure 1–10 *Some modern homes are designed to make use of passive solar-heating systems. Why is the position of the windows important in a passive solar home?*

and washing dishes. Although you may not realize it, between 30 and 50 percent of the energy used in most homes is used to heat water. Solar hot-water systems, which can be used all year round, could save up to 50 percent of the energy cost of heating water. Today, about 800,000 solar hot-water systems are being used in the United States.

Active Solar Heating

An active solar-heating system involves collecting the sun's energy in a device called a **solar collector.** In a typical solar collector, a black surface absorbs energy from the sun and converts it to heat. The surface is covered with glass or plastic panels to trap the heat. Water is heated by pumping it through pipes on the surface. The heated water in the pipes then flows through a storage tank filled with water. Heat is transferred from the water in the pipes to the water in the storage tank. The heated water in the storage tank is pumped throughout the building to provide heat and hot water. At the same time, the water in the pipes returns to the solar collector to be reheated by the sun. You can get a better idea of how an active solar-heating system works by studying Figure 1–11.

Figure 1–11 *Water in a solar collector on the roof of a home is heated by the sun (top). The heat is then transferred in a heat exchanger and used to provide hot water and heat for the home.*

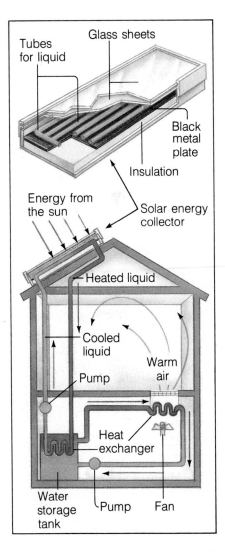

Solar Cells

At the present time, solar-heating systems represent the most common use of solar energy. In the future, however, solar cells may become much more common as sources of usable energy. Solar cells, or **photovoltaic cells,** convert sunlight directly into electricity. (The prefix *photo-* means light, and the suffix *-voltaic* means electrical.) You may be familiar with the use of solar cells in pocket calculators.

A solar cell is a "sandwich" made of extremely thin layers of the element silicon. When sunlight strikes the surface of this sandwich, electrons (negatively charged particles) flow across the layers. This flow of electrons is an electric current, which can be put to work in electric motors or other electrical devices.

Unfortunately, each solar cell produces only a small amount of electricity. A single solar cell can now provide only about 1 watt of electricity—while the sun shines. (The watt is the unit of electric power.) This is about the same amount of power produced by a standard flashlight battery. So large numbers of solar cells are needed to produce useful amounts of electricity. Roof panels consisting of about 5000 solar cells would be needed to provide electricity for an average American home!

Solar cells were first used on a large scale in 1958 to generate electricity aboard the United States satellite *Vanguard I.* Since then, they have been used to generate electricity on many other satellites and spacecraft. Why do you think solar cells would be especially effective in space?

When it comes to providing solar energy for the widest possible use, cost and storage are important considerations. The major disadvantage of solar cells in terms of meeting the everyday electricity needs of homes, schools, and factories has been their cost. In 1959, electricity from solar cells cost about $500 per watt. The cost is now down to about $6 per watt. But it will probably be many years before solar cells

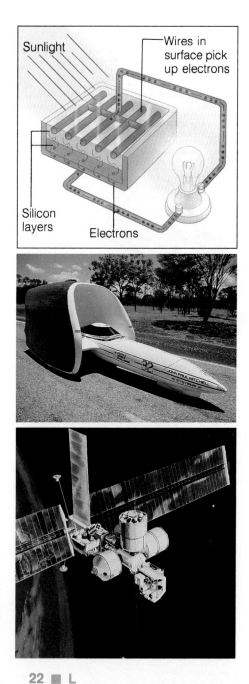

Figure 1–12 *A solar cell, or photovoltaic cell, converts sunlight directly into electricity. A solar-powered car gets all its energy from solar cells. In future space stations, energy will be provided by huge panels of solar cells.*

can compete with the cost of electricity from fossil fuels (about $1 per watt).

Looking further into the future, the National Aeronautics and Space Administration (NASA) has proposed using solar satellites in Earth orbit to provide electricity for people on Earth. These huge panels of solar cells, several kilometers on a side, would be assembled in space. Sunlight falling on the solar panels would produce electricity. The electricity would then be converted to microwaves, a form of radio waves now used in microwave ovens. The microwaves would be beamed to receiving stations on Earth and changed back into electricity for general distribution.

Power Towers

Have you ever used a magnifying glass to focus sunlight onto a spot on a piece of paper or on a leaf? If so, you were probably able to burn a hole through the paper or the leaf. This simple activity illustrates another way of using solar energy. An array of mirrors can be used to focus sunlight onto a boiler mounted on a tower. The sun's heat converts water in the boiler into steam, which drives a turbine to generate electricity. The first such solar plant, called Solar One, is shown in Figure 1–13. Several other similar plants are now being tested. As research continues and new technology is developed, solar energy will probably play an increasingly important role in your life.

Figure 1–13 *In a solar-energy plant, curved mirrors reflect the sun's rays toward a tower of water. Here the heat turns the water into steam, which is used to turn turbines and generate electricity.*

1–2 Section Review

1. What are two uses of solar energy?
2. Briefly describe two types of solar-heating systems.
3. What is a photovoltaic cell? How does it work?

Connection—*You and Your World*

4. In what ways is solar energy now used in your home? Considering the area of the country in which you live, what other uses of solar energy might be appropriate in your home?

1–3 Wind and Water

Throughout history, people have made use of the energy of wind and water. Wind energy has been used to propel sailing ships, turn mill wheels, and pump water from wells. Water mills were once common along thousands of small rivers and streams in the United States, where they were used to grind corn and grain. **Today, the energy of wind and water is used to generate electricity.**

Wind Energy

Winds are caused by the uneven heating of the Earth's atmosphere by the sun. So wind energy can be thought of as an indirect form of solar energy. People have been taking advantage of this readily available source of energy for thousands of years.

Around 1860, small windmills started appearing on farms across the United States. Lightweight, efficient, relatively inexpensive, and easy to install, the early windmills were used to pump water out of the ground. These wind-powered pumps were essential in providing water for crops and farm animals in the farming regions of the Midwest and Southwest.

In 1890, a Danish inventor developed a windmill that could produce small amounts of electricity. American farmers could now enjoy the benefits of electricity provided by their own windmills. Windmill generators were common until the 1930s and 1940s, when transmission lines brought electricity from central power plants to even the most isolated farms.

Figure 1–14 *Windmills on farms are used mainly to pump water. At Altamont Pass in California, thousands of wind generators are used to produce electricity. Why is wind energy considered an indirect form of solar energy?*

As a source of electricity, wind generators were not always reliable. Can you think of some reasons why? They did not work on calm days. And they were easily knocked down or blown apart by strong winds. So when hydroelectric power plants started supplying electricity to rural areas, farmers welcomed the change. The electricity provided by power plants was more dependable than that produced by the wind. By 1950, most wind generators had been abandoned.

But wind energy was not ignored for long! The oil shortages of the early 1970s caused concern about an energy crisis and sparked renewed interest in wind generators. The designs of modern wind generators range from airplane-type propellers to giant "eggbeaters." Designers of large wind generators must select a location where the wind is strong (13 kilometers per hour or more) and blows steadily most of the time. Then they design and build a wind generator to suit that location.

Instead of giant individual wind generators, some developers have built "wind farms" that contain up to several hundred smaller windmills. Today, more than 100 of these wind farms are in operation, and the use of wind energy is growing rapidly. Unfortunately, wind energy will not meet all our energy needs. But some energy planners predict that by the year 2000, almost 10 percent of the electricity generated in the United States will be produced by wind energy. In addition, the increased use of wind energy will save fossil fuels and reduce pollution.

Water Energy

Like wind energy, water energy is an indirect form of solar energy. Energy from the sun causes water to evaporate from lakes and oceans. This water vapor enters the atmosphere and condenses to form clouds. From the clouds, water falls back to the Earth as rain, snow, sleet, or hail. Runoff from rain and melting snow forms rushing streams and rivers, which eventually empty into the oceans—and the cycle continues.

In the late 1700s, water mills in the United States provided energy for machine looms to make cloth or for turning millstones to grind grain. By the 1800s,

Figure 1–15 *For centuries, the mechanical energy of moving water has been used in water mills. Today, falling water at Glen Canyon Dam is used to generate electricity. Is water energy a direct or an indirect form of solar energy?*

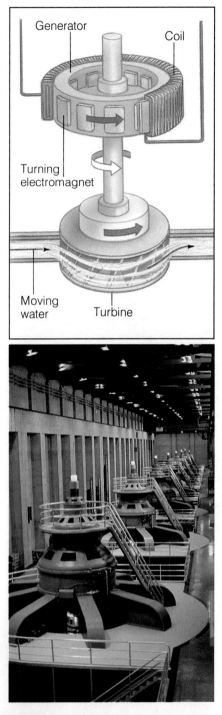

Figure 1-16 *Inside a generator at Hoover Dam, the mechanical energy of moving water spins a turbine. The spinning turbine causes large electromagnets to turn. The turning electromagnets generate electricity.*

most water mills had been replaced by steam engines. But with the invention of the electic light bulb by Thomas Edison in 1879, the demand for electricity increased tremendously. Water energy became important once again as a means of generating electricity.

The use of the mechanical energy of falling or running water to generate usable electricity is called **hydroelectric power.** (The prefix *hydro-* means water.) In a hydroelectric power plant, dams—such as Hoover Dam, which was described at the beginning of this chapter—hold back millions of tons of water in reservoirs. Some of this water is drawn through pipes into the power plant, where it flows through turbines within the plant. The rushing water spins the blades of the turbines, producing electricity in generators. You can see the basic plan and operation of a hydroelectric power plant in Figure 1-16.

Although new hydroelectric power plants are being built, the number of locations in which large dams can be constructed is limited. In this sense, the use of hydroelectric power as a source of energy is limited. In addition, hydroelectric power plants can be somewhat harmful to the environment. For example, patterns of fish migration in rivers may be altered by dams on those rivers. The reservoirs formed behind dams may flood land that might have been used for farming or that might have had great cultural value. For these and other reasons, energy planners do not expect the use of hydroelectric power to increase significantly in the future.

1-3 Section Review

1. Describe how the energy of wind and the energy of water are being used today.
2. Why can both wind energy and water energy be considered indirect forms of solar energy?
3. Why were early wind generators not reliable energy sources?

Critical Thinking—*Making Comparisons*
4. Compare the use of wind generators and hydroelectric power plants in terms of the benefits and problems associated with each.

1–4 Nuclear Energy

As you have read in Section 1–2, life on Earth would not be possible without the energy we receive from the sun. Where does the sun get its energy? The heat and light of the sun (and of all other stars) are produced as a result of reactions taking place deep within the nuclei (NOO-klee-igh; singular, nucleus: NOO-klee-uhs) of atoms. Atoms are the basic building blocks of matter. All objects in the universe are made of matter—and thus of atoms. The **nucleus** is the tiny center of an atom. It is made up of positively charged particles called protons and electrically neutral particles called neutrons. In 1905, Albert Einstein, one of the greatest scientists who ever lived, predicted that if the nucleus of an atom could be split, a new and powerful energy source would be available. This energy, called **nuclear energy,** is the energy locked within the atomic nucleus.

Nuclear Fission

In 1939, **nuclear fission** was discovered. In 1942, the first sustained nuclear fission reaction was carried out by scientists at the University of Chicago. **Nuclear fission is the splitting of an atomic nucleus into two smaller nuclei, during which nuclear energy is released.** Figure 1–18 on page 28 illustrates how a nuclear fission reaction can be made to happen. The diagram shows the most common type of fission reaction, which involves the splitting of a uranium-235 nucleus. (Uranium-235 is a form of the element uranium, containing 92 protons and 143 neutrons in its nucleus.)

To split a uranium-235 nucleus, scientists must shoot a nuclear "bullet" into the nucleus. The nuclear bullet in a fission reaction is a neutron. When a neutron strikes a uranium-235 nucleus, the nucleus is split into two smaller nuclei. During this process, two or more neutrons are released from the uranium-235 nucleus. Energy is released as well.

Each neutron released during a fission reaction is capable of causing another fission reaction by splitting another uranium-235 nucleus. The neutrons released by each of these reactions can then split

Guide for Reading

Focus on this question as you read.

▶ *How is energy released by means of nuclear fission and nuclear fusion?*

Figure 1–17 *An atom consists of a central core, or nucleus, made up of protons and neutrons. A cloud of whirling electrons surrounds the nucleus.*

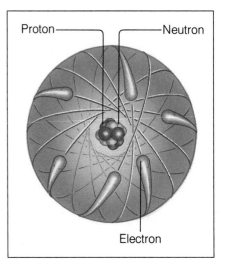

Proton — Neutron

Electron

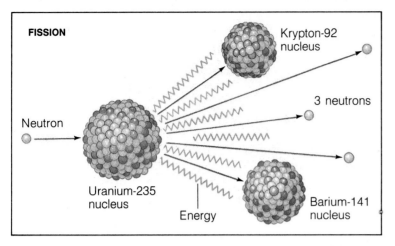

FISSION

Krypton-92 nucleus

Neutron

Uranium-235 nucleus

3 neutrons

Energy

Barium-141 nucleus

Figure 1–18 *In a fission reaction, a uranium-235 nucleus is split by a neutron "bullet." The additional neutrons produced by the fission reaction may cause a nuclear chain reaction. What are the products of a fission reaction?*

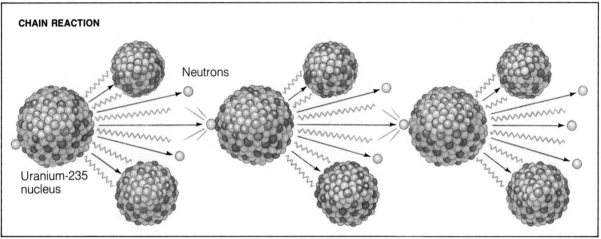

CHAIN REACTION

Neutrons

Uranium-235 nucleus

several more nuclei. In other words, one neutron striking one uranium-235 nucleus starts a chain of nuclear fission reactions. The process in which the splitting of one nucleus causes the splitting of additional nuclei is called a nuclear **chain reaction.**

If a nuclear chain reaction is uncontrolled, the nuclear energy that is released will create a huge explosion. That is just what happens in an atomic bomb. If the chain reaction is carefully controlled, however, the energy that is released can be a valuable energy resource. Controlled nuclear chain reactions take place in nuclear power plants.

Nuclear Power Plants

The energy released during nuclear fission is mostly in the form of heat energy. In a nuclear power plant, this heat energy is used to convert water into steam. The steam then passes through a turbine in an electric generator. The steam spins the blades of the turbine, which produces electricity. So nuclear power plants produce electricity from the energy locked within the nuclei of atoms.

Fission reactions in a nuclear power plant are produced and controlled in a nuclear reactor. The main parts of a nuclear reactor are the containment building and the reactor vessel, which contains the fuel rods and the control rods. Figure 1–19 shows a typical nuclear reactor. Refer to the diagram as you read the description that follows.

The reactor vessel is the central part of a nuclear reactor. It is within the reactor vessel that nuclear fission takes place. To begin a fission reaction, nuclear fuel rods are placed in the reactor vessel. The most common nuclear fuel is uranium-235. When neutrons strike the fuel rods containing pellets of uranium-235, nuclear fission begins. It is important to note that a single nuclear fuel rod does not contain enough uranium-235 to support a chain reaction. Only when many fuel rods are placed close together does a chain reaction occur.

In order for a fission reaction to produce useful energy, the overall speed of the reaction must be

A Model Chain Reaction

1. Line up 15 dominoes to form a triangle as follows. Place 1 domino in the first row. Place 2 dominoes in the second row so that the second row of dominoes is about one half the length of a domino behind the first row. Place 3 dominoes in the third row, 4 in the fourth row, and 5 in the fifth row.

2. Knock over the first domino so that it falls backward. What happens?

3. Set up the dominoes again, but this time remove the second row of dominoes and leave an empty row in its place.

4. Knock over the first domino. What happens this time? How is your model similar to what happens in a nuclear reactor?

■ Why can a chain reaction also be called the "domino effect"?

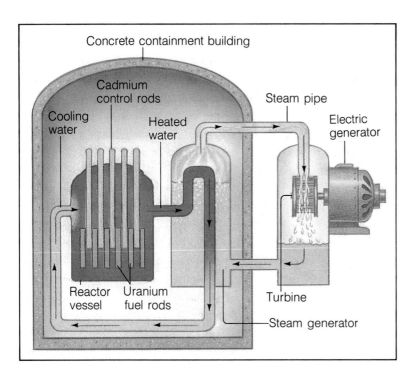

Figure 1–19 *The first nuclear reactor was built under the football stadium at the University of Chicago. This illustration shows the design of a typical modern nuclear reactor. How is the heat produced by a chain reaction converted into electricity?*

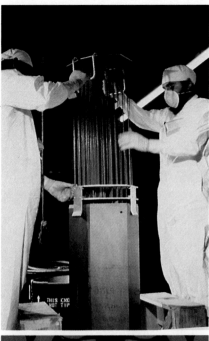

Figure 1–20 *Before being placed in a reactor, nuclear fuel rods are carefully inspected. When the fuel rods are placed at just the right distance from one another, a controlled chain reaction will occur. What is the most common fuel used in nuclear fuel rods?*

carefully controlled. To control the rate of the reaction, neutron-absorbing control rods are placed between the fuel rods. In many reactors, the control rods are made of the element cadmium. When the cadmium control rods are inserted into the reactor, they "soak up" neutrons and slow down the reaction. When the control rods are removed, the fission reaction is speeded up. Thus, the rate of the reaction is controlled by moving the cadmium control rods into or out of the reactor.

Even if a nuclear reactor should get out of control, a nuclear explosion similar to an atomic bomb is impossible. However, it is possible for the reactor to overheat. To prevent the reactor from overheating, water is circulated through the reactor vessel. The hot water from the reactor vessel then passes through a steam generator, where it produces steam to spin a turbine and generate electricity.

Problems With Nuclear Power

At one time, energy planners predicted that nuclear power would become the world's leading source of energy. Just 0.5 kilogram of uranium-235 can produce as much energy as 900 metric tons of coal! And nuclear power does not produce the kinds of pollution caused by burning fossil fuels. Yet predictions of widespread use of nuclear power have not come true. In the United States, only 14 percent of the total electricity generated is produced by nuclear power plants. What went wrong?

Safety is the most obvious concern of many people when they discuss nuclear power. The problem of safety can be divided into four major areas. First, there is the possibility of harmful radiation leaking into the environment. Second, there is the question of what to do with the dangerous radioactive wastes produced by nuclear power plants. Third, there is the possibility of a disastrous meltdown resulting from overheating due to a loss of cooling water in the reactor vessel. And fourth, there is the problem of security; that is, of preventing nuclear fuel from falling into the hands of terrorists.

Aside from the potential safety problems associated with nuclear power plants, the main reason nuclear power has not become a more important energy resource is an economic one. Nuclear power plants are expensive to build. And the electricity produced by nuclear power plants costs more than electricity produced by other energy sources, such as coal.

The problems associated with the use of nuclear power will be discussed more fully in Chapter 3. Scientists are now trying to solve these problems. Will they be able to make nuclear power safer and more cost effective? If they succeed, nuclear power may become a greater source of energy in the future.

Nuclear Fusion

Just as splitting an atomic nucleus releases energy, so does combining two atomic nuclei. **Nuclear fusion is the combining of two atomic nuclei to produce one larger nucleus, with the release of nuclear energy.** In fact, **nuclear fusion** produces far more energy per atom than nuclear fission. Nuclear fusion is the reaction that produces the energy given off by stars such as our sun.

Like other stars, the sun is composed mainly of hydrogen. Within the sun, enormous heat and pressure cause the nuclei of hydrogen atoms to combine, or fuse, into helium nuclei. During this fusion process, some of the mass of the hydrogen is converted into energy. This is the same process that results in the uncontrolled release of nuclear energy in a hydrogen bomb.

To be able to generate useful energy from nuclear fusion, scientists must be able to produce

Figure 1–21 *Three Mile Island nuclear power plant in Pennsylvania was the site of a serious accident in 1979. Radiation escaped into the atmosphere when the reactor's cooling system failed and the reactor overheated.*

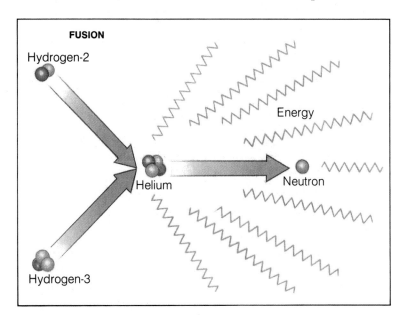

Figure 1–22 *Tremendous amounts of energy are released when two hydrogen nuclei collide to form a helium nucleus. What is this type of nuclear reaction called?*

controlled fusion reactions. If controlled nuclear fusion were practical, it would solve all our energy needs. Because a nuclear fusion reactor would use hydrogen from water, an inexpensive and unlimited supply of fuel would be available. In addition, nuclear fusion would be safer and less polluting than nuclear fission. Unfortunately, scientists have not yet been able to solve the problems involved in producing and sustaining the extremely high temperatures and pressures needed for fusion. Research is continuing, but it will probably be many years before nuclear fusion becomes a practical source of energy.

Figure 1–23 *Scientists at Princeton University are trying to produce a controlled nuclear fusion reaction in this test reactor. If nuclear fusion could be controlled, why would it provide a source of energy that could meet all our future needs?*

1–4 Section Review

1. How is energy released in a nuclear fission reaction? In a nuclear fusion reaction?
2. What is the "bullet" used to start a nuclear fission reaction? Why is the fission reaction that takes place in a nuclear reactor called a chain reaction?
3. What fuel is used in a nuclear fission reaction? In a nuclear fusion reaction?
4. What are the main parts of a nuclear fission reactor? How is the rate of the fission reaction in a nuclear reactor controlled?

Critical Thinking—*Relating Concepts*
5. Why would safe, economical nuclear power provide a good alternative to the use of fossil fuels?

Guide for Reading

Focus on this question as you read.

▶ *What are some alternative energy sources?*

1–5 Alternative Energy Sources

Most of our energy—90 percent—comes from fossil fuels. The remaining 10 percent comes from other energy sources—nuclear, solar, wind, and hydroelectric. Today, there are enough energy sources to meet the world's appetite for energy. For the future, however, alternative energy sources will be needed. Why are these alternative energy sources needed? The answer is twofold. One reason people must look for new, clean sources of energy is pollution. Pollution problems are associated with many energy resources, not just fossil fuels. You will read about some of these pollution problems in Chapter 3.

The other reason people must develop new energy resources is to meet the future energy needs of a growing population. The global population is now more than 5 billion people, and it is expected to reach 6 billion by the year 2000. The present available energy resources cannot be used up today without preparing for tomorrow. Today's generation must use energy wisely to ensure its availability for future generations. **Throughout the world, scientists are working to develop alternative energy sources, such as geothermal energy, tidal energy, biomass, and hydrogen power.**

Geothermal Energy

You may not have realized it, but there is a lot of energy right beneath your feet! **Geothermal energy** is energy produced from the heat energy within the Earth itself. (The word geothermal is made up of the prefix *geo-* meaning Earth and the suffix *-thermal* meaning heat.) The interior of the Earth is extremely hot. Molten (melted) rock deep within the Earth has an average temperature of 1800°C. In some places, the molten rock comes close to the Earth's surface. These places are called hot spots. When water near the Earth's surface comes into contact with these hot spots, the water is heated and bursts forth from the Earth in fountains of steam and boiling water known as geysers. Old Faithful, in Yellowstone National Park, is an example of such a geyser.

In some parts of the world, steam from geysers is used to generate electricity. Steam from geysers can also be used to heat homes, greenhouses, and other buildings directly. In some places, steam is obtained from geothermal wells drilled into reservoirs of hot water.

Hot spots can be used to obtain geothermal energy in another way. Wells can be drilled into hot, dry rock. When water is pumped into these dry wells, the heat in the hot rock turns the water into steam. The steam is then pumped to the surface and

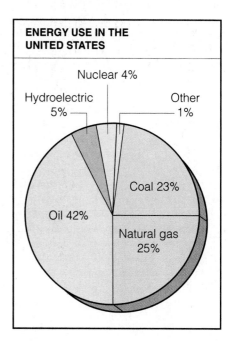

Figure 1–24 *This chart shows the sources of energy used in the United States. How much energy is presently obtained from fossil fuels?*

Dinosaur Power

A dinosaur called *Stegosaurus* roamed the Earth about 150 million years ago. Some scientists believe *Stegosaurus* used solar energy in an unusual way. Find a picture of *Stegosaurus* in a library. Based on the picture, write a hypothesis describing how you think *Stegosaurus* might have used part of its body to absorb solar energy.

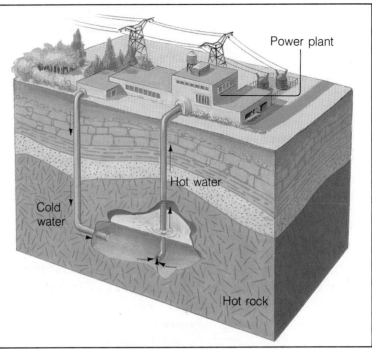

Power plant

Hot water

Cold water

Hot rock

Figure 1–25 *Old Faithful geyser erupts, carrying geothermal energy from deep within the Earth. In a geothermal power plant, cold water is pumped into the Earth, where it is heated, returned to the power plant, and used to generate electricity.*

used to generate electricity or, if the geothermal wells are near a city, to heat homes and other buildings directly.

Geothermal energy is currently being used in Iceland, New Zealand, and parts of the United States, including California and Hawaii. Because the number of hot spots on the Earth is limited, however, geothermal energy is unlikely to keep pace with the world's growing energy needs.

Tidal Energy

Twice a day, the waters of the oceans rise and fall. These high tides and low tides are caused by the gravitational interactions of the sun, the moon, and the Earth. In areas where the difference between high tides and low tides is great, the movement of water can be used as a source of **tidal energy.**

In a tidal power plant, a low dam is built across the entrance to a shallow bay. As the rising and falling tides cause water to flow into and out of the bay, the dam holds back the flow of tidal water. The water then flows past turbines to generate electricity. (This is similar to the way in which electricity is generated in hydroelectric power plants.) Tidal power plants are now in use in France, Canada, and other countries. The use of tidal power as an energy

FIND OUT BY

CALCULATING

Timing the Tides

At Cape May, New Jersey, along the shore of the Atlantic Ocean, there are two high tides every 24 hours and 50 minutes. If the first high tide occurs at 6:00 AM on Tuesday, at what time will it occur on Wednesday? On Thursday?

resource is quite limited, however, since there are relatively few areas in the world where tidal power plants can be built.

Biomass

Any materials that can be burned are said to be combustible. Combustible materials can be used in a variety of ways to produce energy. They can be burned to produce steam, which can then be passed through a turbine to generate electricity. Combustible materials can also be burned to provide heat for homes and factories. The oldest and still most widely used combustible material is wood. Wood is an example of a group of materials known as **biomass.** The term biomass refers to any materials that come from living things. (Remember that wood was once part of a living tree.) Biomass can be burned directly as a fuel or converted into other types of fuels.

DIRECT BURNING Biomass has been burned for cooking and heating purposes for thousands of years. In addition to wood, other forms of biomass are plants and animal wastes. Plants used as biomass fuels include corn husks, sugar cane, sunflowers, and seaweed. In many parts of the world, animal wastes are dried in the sun and used as heating fuel.

Some cities in the United States have recently built power plants that produce steam by burning garbage and other trash. The steam produced in these plants is used directly as a source of heat and hot water or indirectly to generate electricity.

ALCOHOL PRODUCTION Another use of biomass is to produce an alternative fuel to gasoline. Almost all cars in the United States are powered by gasoline. During the gasoline shortages of the 1970s, scientists began looking for alternatives to gasoline. One alternative that was developed is **gasohol.** Gasohol is a mixture of gasoline and alcohol. Ethanol, or ethyl alcohol, is the alcohol that is commonly used in gasohol.

Ethanol is produced by the action of yeast cells on various grains such as corn, wheat, and barley. The yeast cells convert the sugar in the grain into ethanol and carbon dioxide in a process called fermentation (fer-muhn-TAY-shuhn). The use of gasohol was begun in Brazil, which now has large-scale

Figure 1–26 *Sunflowers are combustible materials that can be burned to provide energy. A power plant in California uses discarded automobile tires to generate electricity.*

Figure 1–27 *Gasohol is a fuel that is a mixture of gasoline and alcohol. Where does the alcohol used in gasohol come from?*

Figure 1–28 *Hydrogen gas may someday provide a clean source of energy for automobiles, buses, and other motor vehicles.*

fermentation plants that use sugar cane. Gasohol is widely used in cars in Brazil. Scientists are now experimenting with cars that run entirely on ethanol.

Hydrogen Power

Hydrogen has often been called the "fuel of the future." With the exception of sunlight, hydrogen is the only truly unlimited energy source on Earth. Oceans, rivers, and lakes all contain hydrogen as part of water. Hydrogen gas can be burned in place of fossil fuels such as natural gas. Experimental cars and buses that run on hydrogen gas have been built. And unlike gasoline, the only exhaust from burning hydrogen gas is water!

The problem with using the hydrogen in water is that it is bound to oxygen atoms. A water molecule (H_2O) contains 2 hydrogen atoms bonded to 1 oxygen atom. To obtain hydrogen gas for combustion (burning), a water molecule must be broken down. This is usually done by passing an electric current through water. The process of using electricity to break down water into hydrogen and oxygen is called electrolysis. Electrolysis, however, uses more energy in the form of electricity to produce hydrogen gas than can be obtained by burning hydrogen gas. So at this time, hydrogen power does not appear to be a major alternative energy source.

FIND OUT BY
WRITING

Other Energy Sources

Prepare a report on one of the following energy sources:

Liquid Metal Fast Breeder
 Reactor
Magnetohydrodynamic
 Generators
Ocean Thermal Energy
 Conversion
Fuel Cells
Synfuels
Methane Gas

1–5 Section Review

1. What are four possible alternative energy sources?
2. What is gasohol? How is it produced?
3. What is biomass? Describe two ways of using biomass to produce energy.
4. What is tidal energy? How are tidal power plants similar to hydroelectric power plants?

Connection—*Chemistry*

5. When water is broken down into hydrogen gas and oxygen gas during the process of electrolysis, twice as much hydrogen gas as oxygen gas is produced. Explain this fact using the formula for a water molecule given in this section.

CONNECTIONS

Cold Fusion or ConFusion?

Fusion—the energy that powers the stars—could supply an unlimited source of inexpensive, clean energy. But fusion requires tremendously high temperatures and pressures. *Physicists* have been experimenting with different ways to produce a controlled fusion reaction for nearly 20 years. So far, however, they have not been able to sustain a reaction that produces more energy than is needed to start the reaction.

In 1989, two *chemists* startled the scientific world with a surprising announcement. They claimed to have produced fusion reactions in a simple table-top experiment at room temperature! "Fusion in a bottle"—or cold fusion, as it came to be called—could solve all the world's future energy needs.

Researchers worldwide immediately tried to repeat the original experiment. A National Cold Fusion Research Institute was set up. Hundreds of research papers were published in scientific journals. Although some interesting observations were reported, the results were generally disappointing. More than two years after the first announcement, the existence of cold fusion still had not been confirmed. What was going on?

Some researchers think that the normal procedures of science were ignored because the potential benefits of cold fusion are so great. After all, the first description of cold fusion was given at a press conference, not in a scientific journal. In addition, the two chemists did not share the details of their experimental procedure with researchers trying to duplicate their results.

Still, none of the experiments performed so far have disproved cold fusion. And many researchers are optimistic that they will eventually be able to produce a cold fusion reaction. Research is continuing in the hope that energy from cold fusion may one day be widely available.

Laboratory Investigation

Solar Heating

Problem

How does the color of an object affect the amount of solar energy it absorbs?

Materials *(per group)*

black and white construction paper
tape
scissors
2 metal or plastic containers with plastic lids
2 Celsius thermometers
clock or watch

Procedure 🔬

1. Tape two layers of black paper around one container. Tape two layers of white paper around the other container.

2. Using the scissors, carefully punch a small hole through the center of each lid. Each hole should be large enough to hold a thermometer. **CAUTION:** *Be careful when using scissors.*

3. Fill each container with water at room temperature and cover with a plastic lid.

4. Carefully insert a thermometer through the hole in each lid. Make sure the bulb of the thermometer is below the surface of the water in the container.

5. Place the containers on a sunny windowsill. Be sure each is in direct sunlight.

6. Record the temperature of the water in each container every 3 minutes for 36 minutes. Record your data in a data table.

Observations

1. During which time interval did the temperature in the black container begin to rise? During which time interval did the temperature in the white container begin to rise?

2. What was the final temperature of the water in the black container? In the white container?

3. Make a graph of your data, plotting temperature on the vertical axis and time on the horizontal axis.

Analysis and Conclusions

1. How effectively did the sun's energy heat the water in the containers?

2. Did the color of the containers affect the amount of solar energy they absorbed? Explain your answer.

3. What hidden variable might have affected your results?

4. Based on the results of this experiment, what color clothing would you be likely to wear in the winter? In the summer?

5. **On Your Own**   Design an experiment to test the effects of different colors, such as red, orange, and yellow, on the absorption of solar energy.

Summarizing Key Concepts

1–1 What Are Fossil Fuels?

▲ The three main fossil fuels are coal, oil, and natural gas.

▲ Fossil fuels were formed millions of years ago from the remains of dead plants and animals.

▲ Fossil fuels are used to produce energy for industry, transportation, and home use.

1–2 Energy From the Sun

▲ Life on Earth would not be possible without energy from the sun, or solar energy.

▲ Solar energy is used to heat buildings and to produce electricity.

▲ Solar-heating systems may be either active or passive.

▲ Solar energy is converted directly into electricity by photovoltaic cells.

1–3 Wind and Water

▲ Energy from wind and water can be used to generate electricity.

▲ The use of the energy in moving water to generate electricity is hydroelectric power.

1–4 Nuclear Energy

▲ Nuclear energy is the energy trapped within the nuclei of atoms.

▲ In nuclear fission, energy is released by splitting an atomic nucleus into two smaller nuclei.

▲ In nuclear fusion, energy is released by combining two atomic nuclei into one larger nucleus.

1–5 Alternative Energy Sources

▲ Geothermal energy is produced from heat energy within the Earth.

▲ Tidal energy is produced by the movement of the tides.

▲ Biomass materials, which come from living things, can be used to produce energy.

▲ Hydrogen gas can be burned in place of fossil fuels to produce energy.

Reviewing Key Terms

Define each term in a complete sentence.

1–1 What Are Fossil Fuels?
fossil fuel
hydrocarbon
combustion
peat
lignite
bituminous coal
anthracite
petrochemical

1–2 Energy From the Sun
solar energy
solar collector
photovoltaic cell

1–3 Wind and Water
hydroelectric power

1–4 Nuclear Energy
nucleus
nuclear energy
nuclear fission
chain reaction
nuclear fusion

1–5 Alternative Energy Sources
geothermal energy
tidal energy
biomass
gasohol

Chapter Review

Content Review

Multiple Choice

Choose the letter of the answer that best completes each statement.

1. Wind energy and water energy are both indirect forms of
   a. electric energy.   c. nuclear energy.
   b. solar energy.   d. heat energy.
2. Which of the following is *not* a product made from crude oil?
   a. kerosene   c. gasoline
   b. heating oil   d. oil shale
3. The fuel rods in a nuclear reactor contain pellets of the element
   a. carbon.   c. silicon.
   b. cadmium.   d. uranium.
4. Before being used, solar energy must be converted to other forms of energy because it is
   a. spread out over a wide area.
   b. not available at night.
   c. received mostly in the form of light.
   d. not concentrated in one place.

5. The three main fossil fuels are coal, oil, and
   a. tar sands.   c. hydrogen gas.
   b. natural gas.   d. petroleum.
6. The process by which yeast cells produce alcohol from biomass materials is called
   a. combustion.   c. fermentation.
   b. electrolysis.   d. fusion.
7. Solar cells, or photovoltaic cells, are made of thin layers of the element
   a. carbon.   c. silicon.
   b. uranium.   d. hydrogen.
8. Which of the following is a problem associated with the use of nuclear power?
   a. possible radiation leaks
   b. storing radioactive wastes
   c. meltdown due to overheating
   d. all of these

True or False

If the statement is true, write "true." If it is false, change the underlined word or words to make the statement true.

1. In a nuclear <u>fission</u> reaction, two hydrogen nuclei combine to form a helium nucleus.
2. Large windmills <u>cannot</u> be used to generate electricity.
3. The "bullet" used to start a nuclear chain reaction is a <u>proton</u>.
4. The form of coal that is almost pure carbon is <u>lignite</u>.
5. The alcohol that is mixed with gasoline to produce gasohol is <u>ethanol</u>.
6. Most of the energy used in this country comes from <u>alternative energy sources</u>.
7. A backup heating system usually <u>is not</u> needed in a passive solar home.

Concept Mapping

Complete the following concept map for Section 1–1. Refer to pages L6–L7 to construct a concept map for the entire chapter.

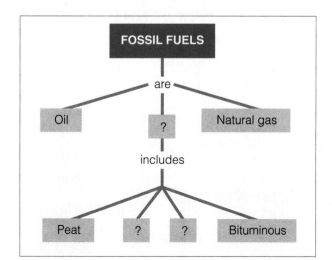

Concept Mastery

Discuss each of the following in a brief paragraph.

1. Discuss the advantages and disadvantages of solar cells.
2. Describe the four stages in the development of coal.
3. Describe how a nuclear fission reaction is controlled in a nuclear reactor.
4. Explain what is meant by a nuclear chain reaction.
5. Compare the benefits and risks of nuclear fission and nuclear fusion as a source of energy.
6. Trace the use of wind energy in the United States from 1860 to the present.
7. Describe two uses of biomass as a source of energy.
8. Explain why the use of geothermal energy, hydroelectric power, and tidal power is limited.

Critical Thinking and Problem Solving

Use the skills you have developed in this chapter to answer each of the following.

1. **Making calculations** The population of the United States is approximately 250 million people. For each person, approximately 35 kilograms of fossil fuels are consumed every day. How much fossil fuel is used in the United States every day? Every month? Every year?
2. **Making observations** Keep a list of the ways in which you use energy every day for a period of several days. Be sure to identify the source of each type of energy used. Are there any ways in which you could have reduced your use of energy?
3. **Making maps** Choose either geothermal energy or tidal power. Find out where in the world these energy resources are located. Identify these locations on a world map.
4. **Making predictions** Some states, such as Texas, Louisiana, and Alabama, depend on oil and natural gas reserves for much of their income. What do you think might happen to the economy of these states if the oil and natural gas reserves were used up? How do you think this could be prevented from happening?
5. **Interpreting diagrams** Describe what is happening in this diagram. What is this process called?

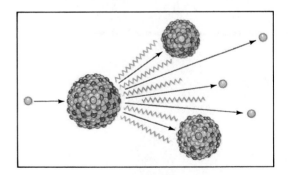

6. **Using the writing process** Write an essay explaining why you agree or disagree with the following statement: The United States should abandon the use of nuclear reactors as a source of energy and concentrate on developing alternative energy sources.

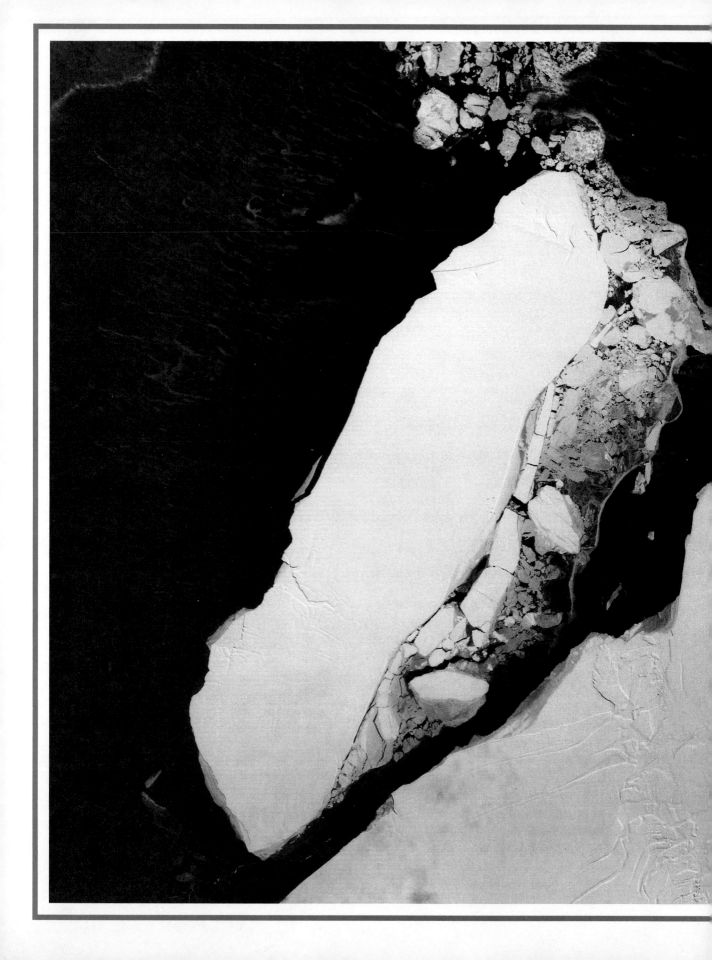

Earth's Nonliving Resources

Guide for Reading

After you read the following sections, you will be able to

2-1 Land and Soil Resources
- Identify ways in which people use land and soil resources.
- Define erosion and describe some methods of preventing erosion.

2-2 Water Resources
- Relate freshwater supplies to people's needs.

2-3 Mineral Resources
- Identify common metallic and nonmetallic minerals.

Like a ghostly floating island, a huge iceberg drifts through the polar ocean past the frozen coast of Antarctica. The floating island of ice—154 kilometers long, 35 kilometers wide, and 225 meters deep—broke away from Antarctica's Ross Ice Shelf in 1987. Before splitting up into three smaller pieces in 1990, the mountainous iceberg floated a distance of 2000 kilometers. Scientists tracking the iceberg estimated that it contained enough fresh water to provide everyone on Earth with two glasses of water a day for the next 1977 years!

Almost 3 percent of the Earth's freshwater supply is locked up in the ice at the North and South poles. Antarctica alone contains about 90 percent of the world's ice. Might we someday be using this ice as a source of fresh water? Where does most of our drinking water come from today? You will find the answers to these questions as you read this chapter about the Earth's nonliving resources. You will also learn about some of the Earth's other nonliving resources—land, soil, and minerals.

Journal *Activity*

You and Your World Are you a "water waster"? In your journal, keep a record of all the ways in which you use water every day. Identify the ways in which you may be wasting water. Then make a list of ways in which you might be able to use less water every day. (No, skipping a shower or not brushing your teeth doesn't count!)

Icebergs are large chunks of ice that break off glaciers and drift into the oceans. Do you think icebergs may someday provide a source of fresh water?

2–1 Land and Soil Resources

More than 5 billion people now inhabit the Earth. Everything people need to survive must come from the Earth itself. In fact, the Earth is like a giant storehouse of useful materials. Materials removed from the Earth and used by people are called **natural resources**. The fossil fuels—coal, oil, and natural gas—you read about in Chapter 1 are examples of the Earth's natural resources. Natural resources are the riches of the Earth. They provide a treasure chest of materials that improve our lives. And they are the inheritance we will leave to our children and grandchildren.

Scientists divide the Earth's natural resources into two groups. One group is the **nonrenewable resources**. These resources cannot be replaced by nature. Fossil fuels are nonrenewable resources. Once they are gone, they cannot be replaced. Minerals, such as copper and iron, are also nonrenewable resources. They are not replaced by nature. Mineral resources are discussed in Section 2–3.

The other group of natural resources is the **renewable resources**. Renewable resources can be replaced by nature. Wood is a renewable resource because forests can be replanted. Water is a renewable resource because it is constantly replaced by rain, snow, sleet, and hail. You will learn more about the Earth's water resources in the following section.

Figure 2–1 *All the natural resources humans need to survive—land, water, and minerals—come from the Earth. Is land a renewable or a nonrenewable resource?*

Soil, too, is a renewable resource because new soil is formed on the Earth every day. Soil formation, however, is an extremely slow process. Although land and soil resources are renewable, nature may take anywhere from a few decades to several million years to replace land and soil that have been lost.

Land Use

One third of the Earth's surface—about 13 billion hectares—is covered by land. But only a portion of this land can be used for farming or for living space. All land is not suitable for all uses. **Land is used for cities, highways, forests, farms, and pastures.** And even though a growing population needs more and more land, it is a limited resource. As the American writer and humorist Mark Twain said about land, "They don't make it anymore."

Land is needed for building cities and towns to house the increasing human population. Land is also needed for industry and for farming. These needs must be carefully weighed and balanced. If too much land is used for cities, there may not be enough left for farms. But both uses are important.

An increasing population requires an increase in food production. The Earth's farmland must be used to its fullest potential. New and improved crop varieties must be developed. Better growing methods must be used to make existing farms more productive.

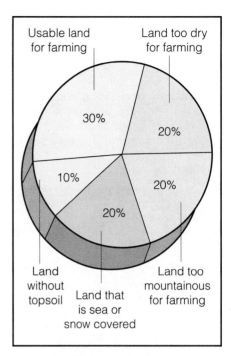

Figure 2–2 *Land is a valuable resource that is used for many purposes. What percentage of the Earth's land is used for farming?*

Figure 2–3 *Land that is too dry for farming may be irrigated or it may be used as grazing land for cattle. These pigs are enjoying a hearty barnyard meal. Where does the food used to feed pigs and other farm animals come from?*

Figure 2–4 *Nodules, or lumps, of nitrogen-fixing bacteria grow on the roots of soybean plants. How do farmers use crops such as clover to prevent depletion of nutrients from the soil?*

And land that is now unusable for farming must be made fertile. One way to do this is by **irrigation** (ihr-uh-GAY-shuhn). Irrigation is the process of supplying water to dry regions. As a result of irrigation, regions that do not have enough water for crops can be made suitable for farming.

Land is also needed for raising animals. Pigs, sheep, chickens, and cattle are renewable resources. But they must be fed. An enormous amount of farmland is used to grow food for animals. For example, more than 10 kilograms of grain are required to produce only 1 kilogram of beef from a steer! In fact, about 30 percent of all the grain grown in the world is used to feed livestock (farm animals). And land that is used as pasture or open range for grazing animals cannot be used to grow crops at all.

Land Management

If limited land resources are to be preserved, land use must be carefully planned and managed. Different land areas are best suited for different purposes. For example, some land areas are best for growing trees. Other land areas are best used as pastures for cattle and sheep. Areas that can produce the best crops should become farmland. Recreational areas should be carefully developed so as not to damage nearby farmlands and forests. Cities, towns, and factories should be built in areas where the least harm will be done to the environment. What do you think happens when cities are built without careful planning?

Even farming must be a planned activity. Crops use up nutrients (NOO-tree-uhnts) in the soil. Nutrients are chemical substances necessary for plant growth. When one type of crop is grown on the same land for too long, **depletion** may result. Depletion occurs when nutrients are removed from the soil. Corn, for example, removes nitrogen from the soil. Certain crops naturally put back nutrients that others remove. Crops such as clover and peanuts put nitrogen back into the soil. So farmers alternate crops on the same land each year. They may plant a nitrogen-using crop, such as corn, one year and a nitrogen-producing crop, such as clover, the next. This method of farming is called **crop rotation**.

Figure 2–5 *Two methods of preventing erosion are contour plowing (left) and strip cropping (right). What are two cover crops often used in strip cropping?*

Crop rotation keeps nutrients in the soil from being depleted. Why is this important?

Two other good land-management practices are **contour plowing** and **strip cropping**. Contour plowing involves planting crops across the face of a slope of land instead of up and down the slope. See Figure 2–5. In strip cropping, farmers plant strips of low cover crops between strips of other crops. Cover crops are crops that completely cover the soil. They help to hold down the soil between other crops. Hay and wheat are two common cover crops that are often planted between rows of corn.

Erosion

Growing crops is one of the most important uses of soil. Crops are grown in topsoil, which is the rich upper layer of soil. It can take anywhere from 200 to 400 years to form 1 centimeter of topsoil. In many areas, topsoil is being lost because of **erosion**. Erosion is the carrying off of soil by water or wind. Although erosion is a natural process, poor land-management practices can speed up its rate. Worldwide, topsoil is being lost up to ten times faster than new soil is being formed.

Both contour plowing and strip cropping can prevent erosion. Another method for preventing erosion is called **terracing**. Terracing is plowing a

Figure 2–6 *To prevent soil erosion due to water running down the sides of a hill in Bali, the hill has been plowed into a series of level steps. What is this method of plowing called?*

slope into a series of level steps, or terraces, for planting. The use of terracing and contour plowing on slopes slows down the runoff of water after heavy rains or from melting snow. Both methods help prevent the water from rushing downhill and carrying away valuable topsoil.

To prevent erosion due to wind, farmers often plant windbreaks. Windbreaks are rows of trees planted between fields of crops. The trees act as a barrier to help prevent topsoil from being blown away by the wind.

Some regions are too dry for crops to be grown, but they can support grasslands. These grasslands have traditionally been used for grazing animals, such as cattle and sheep. If there are too many animals on the land, however, they may eat all the available grasses. This results in overgrazing the land. Overgrazing leaves the topsoil exposed to wind erosion. As a result of erosion caused by overgrazing, dry grasslands become deserts. This process is called **desertification** (dih-zert-ih-fih-KAY-shuhn). Desertification is taking place all over the world, even in parts of the United States. The United States Bureau of Land Management has estimated that an area of land the size of Utah is currently in danger of desertification because of overgrazing.

FIND OUT BY
CALCULATING

Erosion Losses

It has been estimated that the Earth loses 1.8 billion kilograms of soil to erosion every year. How many kilograms of soil are lost in 5 years? In 10 years?

Figure 2-7 *A woman in Zimbabwe, Africa, carries a load of firewood. Cutting down trees for firewood speeds up soil erosion and may lead to desertification.*

Land and Soil Reclamation

Sometimes valuable land resources must be disturbed to get at resources of fossil fuels or minerals below the surface. Coal just beneath the surface of the land often can be removed only by strip mining. In strip mining, huge power shovels dig up the land above the coal and remove the coal. But this does not necessarily mean that the land must be destroyed forever. It may be possible for the land to be reclaimed, or restored to its original condition.

Land reclamation involves several steps. First, the valuable topsoil is carefully removed and stored. Then the less valuable layers of soil beneath the topsoil are stripped away. The coal, which is now exposed, is removed and shipped to coal-processing plants. During this procedure, the disturbed soil must be protected from erosion, and water in the area must be monitored to make sure it does not become chemically polluted. After all the coal has been mined, the layers of soil and the topsoil are put back in place. The final step in land reclamation is seeding and planting the land. Although strip mining is not as destructive as it once was, it still has harmful effects on the land. What do you think some of these effects are?

FIND OUT BY READING

The Ethics of Land Use

Often, making decisions about land use is not easy. In his book *The Sand County Almanac,* published in the 1940s, Aldo Leopold pointed out the need for a land ethic. An ethic is a system of values by which decisions are made and on which actions are based. Leopold called for an ethic by which decisions about land use are based on the ecological value of land resources.

Figure 2–8 *Mining coal just beneath the surface of the land causes ugly scars on the land. But the land can be reclaimed and returned to its natural beauty. What is this kind of coal mining called?*

2–1 Section Review

1. What are some ways in which people use land and soil resources?
2. What is the difference between renewable and nonrenewable resources? Name at least two nonrenewable and two renewable resources.
3. Describe two farming methods that help prevent soil erosion due to water runoff.
4. Why is it important to prevent overgrazing of grasslands?

Critical Thinking—*Making Predictions*

5. Predict how an increase in population will affect land use in the future.

Guide for Reading

Focus on this question as you read.

▶ *Why is it important to preserve supplies of fresh water?*

2–2 Water Resources

"Water, water everywhere" is probably the first thought that comes to mind when you look at a photograph of the Earth from space. As the science fiction writer Arthur C. Clarke has pointed out, although our planet is called Earth, it might just as well be called Water. In fact, there are 1520 billion billion liters of water above, on, and in the Earth! The problem is that only a small percentage of this vast water resource is available for use by people. **Even though water is a renewable resource, there is a limited supply of fresh water.** Most of the Earth's water—97 percent—is in the oceans. But ocean water cannot be used for drinking, irrigation, or industrial processes. Do you know why? You are correct if you said because it is too salty.

Uses of Water

In the United States, billions of liters of water are used every day. The chart in Figure 2–10 shows the estimated daily use of water for an average American family of four. Each person drinks about 1.5 liters of water per day. People also need water for other uses, such as bathing, cooking, and cleaning. It has been estimated that each person in the United States uses more than 400 liters of water daily! Based on this estimate, what would be the total amount of water used by your class in one year?

In the United States, industry uses more than 10 billion liters of water every day. And it takes more than 375 billion liters of water per day to irrigate farmlands in the southern and western United States. Where do you think this water comes from?

Figure 2–9 *Without water, life on Earth would be impossible. But most of the Earth's water is in the oceans. And ocean water is too salty to be used for drinking or for irrigation.*

Figure 2–10 *According to the graph, about how much water does a family of four use for bathing every day?*

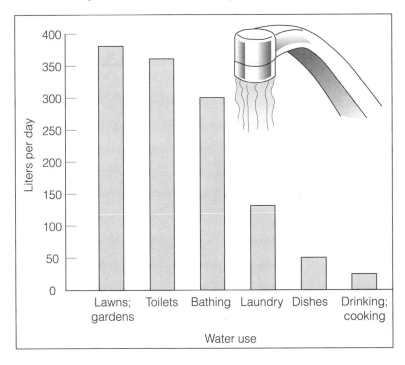

The Water Cycle

The Earth's supply of fresh water is constantly being renewed by means of the **water cycle**. A cycle is a continuous, repeating chain of events. The water cycle is the movement of water from the Earth's surface to the atmosphere (the envelope of air surrounding the Earth) and back to the surface. Three basic steps make up the water cycle. Refer to the diagram in Figure 2–11 as you read the description that follows.

In the first step of the water cycle, water on the Earth's surface is heated by the sun and evaporates (changes from a liquid to a gas). This gas, or water vapor, then rises into the atmosphere. As water vapor rises into the upper atmosphere, the vapor cools, condenses (changes from a gas to a liquid), and forms clouds. This is the second step of the water cycle. During the third step of the water cycle, the water falls back to the surface of the Earth as precipitation—rain, snow, sleet, or hail. Most precipitation falls directly into oceans, lakes, rivers,

Figure 2–11 *The water cycle constantly renews Earth's supply of fresh water. What happens to the water that falls to Earth as precipitation?*

WATER CYCLE

Water vapor condenses, forming clouds

Water falls to Earth as precipitation

Precipitation runs off into bodies of water

Surface water evaporates

Precipitation soaks into ground, becoming groundwater

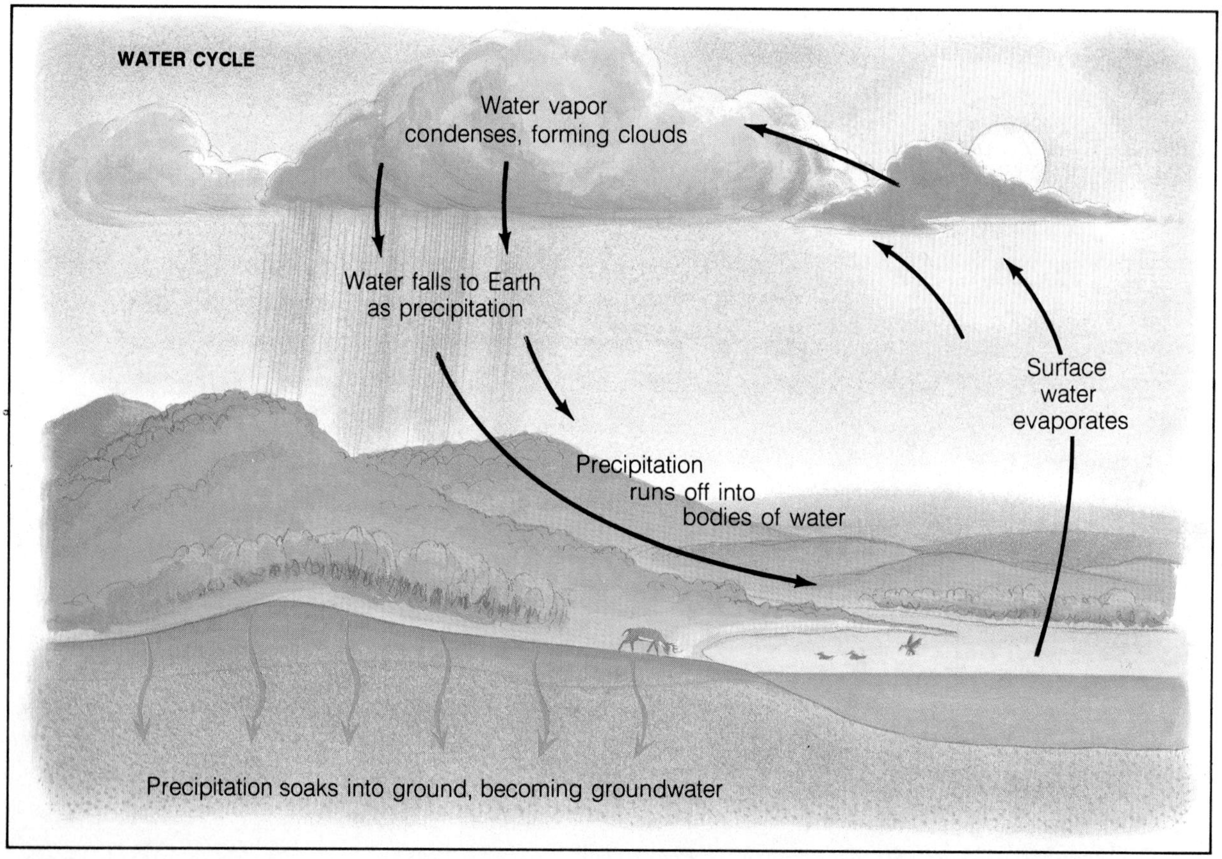

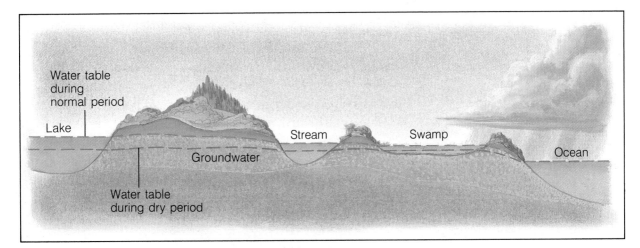

Figure 2–12 *Water that is stored in the soil is called groundwater. The level below which the soil is soaked with water is called the water table. As you can see in the diagram, the water table follows the shape of the land.*

and streams. Some precipitation falls onto the land and runs off into these bodies of water. Eventually, the water returns to the atmosphere through evaporation, and the cycle continues.

Sources of Fresh Water

Most of the Earth's water resources are in oceans, lakes, rivers, and streams. Water is also found in the soil as **groundwater** and frozen as ice in glaciers and polar icecaps. As you know, water in the oceans is too salty to be used. And the ice in glaciers is not directly available. So the main sources of fresh water for human use are groundwater, freshwater lakes, and rivers.

More than 300 billion liters of groundwater are taken out of the ground daily in this country, mostly for use on farms and in factories. Half of the drinking water in the United States comes from groundwater. Although the United States has a plentiful supply of groundwater, it takes hundreds of years for large amounts of groundwater to accumulate. In many parts of the country, groundwater is being used up faster than it is being replaced. As a result, the level of groundwater is dropping and lakes and rivers may eventually dry up. Wells must be drilled deeper and deeper as the groundwater level drops. Where can we turn for new sources of fresh water?

Figure 2–13 *A severe drought, or dry period, may cause reservoirs and other sources of fresh water to dry up.*

FIND OUT BY WRITING

Some Words About Water

The following terms can be used to describe water:

> water quality
> fresh water
> salt water
> brackish water
> hard water
> soft water
> polluted water
> purified water

Using reference materials in the library, find out what each term means.

New Sources of Fresh Water

An abundant supply of fresh water can be made available by **desalination** (dee-sal-uh-NAY-shuhn) of ocean water. Desalination is the process by which salt is removed from ocean water. (The word salt comes from the Latin word *sal*.) Some cities in the United States, such as Key West, Florida, and Freeport, Texas, have already built desalination plants. The desalination plants supply these cities with more than 20 million liters of fresh water daily. Other plants are planned for California, which has a serious shortage of fresh water.

What about the fresh water locked in the ice of glaciers? Is there any way to obtain this water for human use? In fact, some scientists have suggested that it might be possible to tow icebergs from around the poles to large coastal cities in the United States. Once there, the icebergs could be mined for fresh water. Scientists are not sure, however, what effects such a project might have on the environment.

In order to have enough usable fresh water in the future, harmful substances and dangerous organisms must be removed from our water supplies. The problem of water pollution is discussed in detail in Chapter 3. In addition, everyone must learn to use our limited sources of fresh water wisely. You will learn more about the importance of safeguarding our water resources in Chapter 4.

Figure 2–14 *Yuma, Arizona, in the middle of a desert, gets some of its fresh water from a desalination plant. Most of the Earth's fresh water is frozen in glaciers.*

Oil in the Soil

What do you think of when you hear the words oil spill? You probably have an image of a large black oil slick floating on the surface of the ocean or of beaches covered with gooey tar. Most oil spills do fit these descriptions. But there is another kind of oil spill that can be just as damaging although it usually receives little or no publicity. This type of oil spill occurs underground.

Unlike dramatic above-ground oil spills, underground oil spills are usually slow leaks that may take years to be noticed. Most underground spills come from leaks in underground petroleum storage tanks, gas station tanks, or home-heating-oil tanks. Some underground oil spills have been known to exist for years, even decades. But it is only recently that the danger of these spills has been recognized.

Making Inferences

1. What do you think is the danger of underground oil spills? (*Hint:* Where does most of our drinking water come from?)

2. Do you think underground oil spills are more difficult to clean up than above-ground oil spills?

2–2 Section Review

1. Why might it be necessary to find new sources of fresh water?
2. About how much water does each person in the United States use daily?
3. What is a cycle? Trace the sequence of steps in the water cycle.
4. What are the main sources of fresh water now used by people? What are some possible new sources of fresh water?

Connection—*You and Your World*

5. Using Figure 2–10, estimate the amount of water you use daily. Suppose a water shortage existed in your region and people were asked to decrease their use of water by 25 percent. How would you cut back on your water use?

Guide for Reading

*Focus on this question as
you read.*

▶ *What are some common
metallic and nonmetallic
minerals?*

2–3 Mineral Resources

Since the dawn of human civilization, people have used materials from the Earth to make tools. Archaeologists have uncovered primitive tools from the Stone Age, the Iron Age, and the Bronze Age. Even the names given to these periods in human history reflect the importance of toolmaking and of the materials used to make the tools. Many of these materials are even more important in today's modern technological society.

In this textbook, a **mineral** is defined as a naturally occurring chemical substance found in soil or rocks. Today, minerals are used to make a variety of products, from aluminum cans to silver jewelry. Minerals are nonrenewable resources. Why do you think minerals are considered nonrenewable resources?

Minerals are either metallic or nonmetallic. **Metallic minerals include copper, iron, and aluminum. Nonmetallic minerals include quartz, limestone, and sulfur.** The chart in Figure 2–15 lists some common metallic and nonmetallic minerals. Both metallic and nonmetallic minerals are important natural resources.

Ores

To obtain a useful mineral, the mineral must be mined, or removed from the Earth. Deposits of

Figure 2–15 *The chart lists some important metallic and nonmetallic minerals. What is the mineral potash used for?*

SOME IMPORTANT MINERAL RESOURCES			
Nonmetallic		**Metallic**	
Mineral	**Use**	**Mineral**	**Use**
Calcite	Cement	Hematite	Cast iron
Quartz	Watches	Bauxite	Aluminum cans
Sulfur	Chemicals	Argentite	Silver jewelry
Halite	Salt	Cuprite	Copper wire
Potash	Fertilizer	Rutile	Titanium aircraft parts
Clay	Brick	Wolframite	Tungsten steel

minerals that can be mined at a profit are called **ores**. If the percentage of a mineral in an ore is high, the ore is called a high-grade ore. If the percentage of the mineral is low, the ore is called a low-grade ore. Ores are found all over the Earth. Do you know of any ores that are mined in your state?

The Earth's crust is a storehouse of mineral riches. Iron is the most widely used metal extracted from metallic ores. Other elements, including chromium, nickel, and carbon, can be added to iron to produce steel. Steel is an **alloy**, or a substance made of two or more metals. By combining various amounts of chromium, nickel, and carbon with iron, different alloys of steel with different properties can be made. Chromium is added in the steelmaking process to provide resistance to rusting. A low percentage of carbon results in very soft steel, such as that used in paper clips.

Other metals removed from metallic ores include copper, which is used in electric wires, and aluminum, which is used in cans. Gold and silver, used in jewelry, are also found in metallic ores. What other metals do you use in your daily life?

Figure 2–16 *Simple tools made of copper were used by the people of Peru thousands of years ago. Where did they obtain the copper to make the tools?*

Mining and Processing Ores

Once mineral deposits have been located, they must be mined. Unfortunately, the only practical way to obtain most minerals—especially from low-grade ores—is through open-pit mining. And open-pit mining can have disastrous effects on land and groundwater resources. You will learn more about

Figure 2–17 *Copper, which is obtained from open-pit mines, is today used to make wire, pipes, and nails. One common source of copper is the mineral bornite.*

Figure 2–18 *Potato-sized nodules of the mineral manganese are found on the ocean floor.*

the problems associated with open-pit mining, or strip mining, in Chapter 3.

Mining the ore is only the first step in obtaining a useful mineral. To extract the mineral from the ore, impurities in the ore are removed. A purified mineral remains. Then the mineral is processed so that it can be sent to manufacturing plants in a usable form. At the manufacturing plant, the mineral is used to make the final product.

Mining the Oceans

The minerals in the Earth's crust have been formed over millions, or even billions, of years. The Earth contains only a limited amount of the minerals used today. The mining of minerals cannot continue at its present rate or we will run out of minerals. What is the answer to this dilemma? One answer is to recycle, or reuse, minerals. Another is to find other materials to take their place in the products we use. You will learn more about these options in Chapter 4.

Another possibility is to search for minerals in the last unexplored place on Earth—the ocean floor. Deposits of manganese, nickel, cobalt, and perhaps copper have already been located on the ocean floor. If these deposits can be mined economically, they may provide a valuable new source of mineral resources.

FIND OUT BY

From the Earth

Many of the items you use every day are made from minerals. For the next 24 hours, record each item you use that is made from minerals. Using library reference materials, determine which minerals may soon be in short supply and which appear to be plentiful. Present your findings in the form of a bulletin board display.

2–3 Section Review

1. Name three metallic and three nonmetallic minerals.
2. What is the difference between an ore and an alloy?
3. Trace the sequence of steps involved in mining and processing an ore.
4. What are some minerals that might someday be mined from the ocean floor?

Connection—*Life Science*

5. What are some ways in which fishes and other living things in the ocean might be affected by large-scale mining of the ocean floor?

CONNECTIONS

Washing Away History

Not all erosion takes place on farmland or grazing land. Today, the United States is in danger of losing 90 percent of its coastline to erosion caused by ocean waves. One of the most visible victims of this threatened erosion is the historic 110-year-old Cape Hatteras Lighthouse located on the Outer Banks of North Carolina. The lighthouse, which was built in 1870, once stood at a safe distance of 450 meters from the pounding surf. Today the distance has shrunk to 90 meters. One big Atlantic storm could wash the lighthouse into the sea!

What can be done to save the Cape Hatteras Lighthouse? Geologists, engineers, and environmentalists disagree on the answer. The National Park Service has approved a suggestion to move the lighthouse back to a safe distance from the ocean. The U.S. Army Corps of Engineers has come up with a plan to build a series of protective structures around the lighthouse. Some environmental groups, however, are in favor of letting nature takes its course and sacrificing the lighthouse to the sea. But it may not be just the lighthouse that is sacrificed. In addition to the lighthouse, the fate of a nearby wildlife refuge as well as North Carolina's profitable tourist industry are at stake. What course of action would you choose?

Laboratory Investigation

Erosion by Raindrops

Problem

How can raindrops splashing against bare soil cause erosion?

Materials *(per group)*

2 petri dishes	meterstick
silt	medicine dropper
2 sheets of paper	sod

Procedure 🧪 👁

1. Fill one petri dish with silt to a depth of about 1 cm. Make sure the surface of the silt is smooth and level.

2. Place the petri dish in the center of a large sheet of paper.

3. Hold the meterstick next to the petri dish. Using the medicine dropper, allow a drop of water to fall from a height of 1 meter onto the surface of the silt. Observe what happens to the silt. **CAUTION:** *Wear your safety goggles.*

4. Measure the greatest distance in centimeters that the silt splashed from the dish. Record the distance in a data table.

5. Repeat steps 3 and 4 two more times. Calculate the average distance the silt splashed from the dish. Record the average distance in the data table.

6. Place a small piece of sod in the second petri dish. Repeat steps 2 through 5.

Observations

1. What happened to the silt in the petri dish when it was hit by a water drop? What happened to the sod?

2. What was the average splash distance from the dish with the silt? From the dish with the sod?

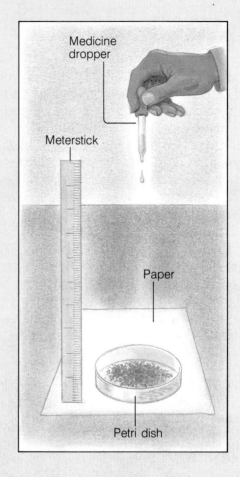

Analysis and Conclusions

1. How did using sod instead of silt affect the splash distance? Explain.

2. Erosion caused by raindrops striking bare soil is called splash erosion. Why is this an appropriate name for this type of erosion?

3. Would overgrazing of grasslands increase or decrease the likelihood of splash erosion? Explain.

4. **On Your Own**   How are different types of soil affected by splash erosion? Repeat this investigation using different types of soil, such as coarse sand, clay, fine gravel, and potting soil. Compare your results with the results of this investigation.

Summarizing Key Concepts

2-1 Land and Soil Resources

△ Materials removed from the Earth and used by people are called natural resources.

△ Scientists divide natural resources into two groups: renewable resources and nonrenewable resources.

△ Renewable resources can be replaced by nature, whereas nonrenewable resources cannot.

△ Although land and soil are renewable resources, anywhere from decades to millions of years are required to replace land and soil that have been lost.

△ Land use must be carefully planned and managed.

△ Strip cropping, contour plowing, terracing, and windbreaks can help prevent soil erosion.

△ Depletion of nutrients in the soil can be prevented by crop rotation.

△ Land that has been damaged by strip mining may be reclaimed, or restored to its original condition.

2-2 Water Resources

△ Although water is a renewable resource, there is a limited supply of fresh water.

△ The Earth's supply of fresh water is constantly being renewed by means of the water cycle.

△ The main sources of fresh water are groundwater, freshwater lakes, and rivers.

△ Half the drinking water in the United States comes from groundwater.

△ Fresh water can be produced from ocean water by the process of desalination.

2-3 Mineral Resources

△ A mineral is a natural substance found in soil or rocks.

△ Deposits of minerals that can be profitably mined are called ores.

△ An alloy is a substance that combines two or more metals.

△ It may be possible to obtain certain minerals from deposits located on the ocean floor.

Reviewing Key Terms

Define each term in a complete sentence.

2-1 Land and Soil Resources
natural resource
nonrenewable resource
renewable resource
irrigation
depletion
crop rotation
contour plowing
strip cropping

erosion
terracing
desertification

2-2 Water Resources
water cycle
groundwater
desalination

2-3 Mineral Resources
mineral
ore
alloy

Chapter Review

Content Review

Multiple Choice

Choose the letter of the answer that best completes each statement.

1. Which of the following is a nonrenewable resource?
   a. copper   c. soil
   b. water   d. wood
2. Plowing the land across the face of a slope is called
   a. terracing.
   b. contour plowing.
   c. crop rotation.
   d. strip cropping.
3. A natural substance found in soil or rocks is called a(an)
   a. crop.
   b. mineral.
   c. alloy.
   d. strip mine.
4. Which of the following is a metallic mineral?
   a. sulfur   c. quartz
   b. copper   d. limestone

5. In the United States, the percentage of drinking water supplied by groundwater is
   a. 25 percent.   c. 75 percent.
   b. 50 percent.   d. 100 percent.
6. The process by which nutrients are removed from the soil is called
   a. erosion.   c. depletion.
   b. crop rotation. d. desertification.
7. Most of the Earth's water is found in
   a. rivers.   c. lakes.
   b. groundwater.   d. oceans.
8. Erosion due to wind can be prevented by
   a. irrigation.   c. terracing.
   b. windbreaks.   d. overgrazing.
9. The process by which salt is removed from ocean water is called
   a. desalination.   c. purification.
   b. cloud seeding. d. irrigation.

True or False

If the statement is true, write "true." If it is false, change the underlined word or words to make the statement true.

1. <u>Renewable</u> resources cannot be replaced once they are used up.
2. Rock deposits that contain minerals mined at a profit are called <u>ores</u>.
3. Wood, soil, and water are examples of <u>nonrenewable</u> resources.
4. Restoring the land to its original condition after resources have been mined is called land <u>management</u>.
5. The first step of the water cycle involves <u>evaporation</u>.
6. The process by which grasslands are turned into deserts as a result of wind erosion is called <u>terracing</u>.

Concept Mapping

Complete the following concept map for Section 2–1. Refer to pages L6–L7 to construct a concept map for the entire chapter.

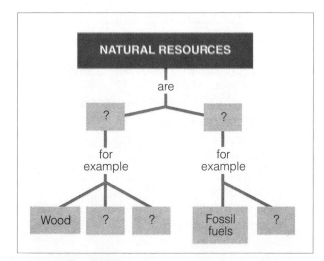

Concept Mastery

Discuss each of the following in a brief paragraph.

1. In what ways does an increase in population affect land and water resources?
2. Compare renewable and nonrenewable natural resources. Give at least two examples of each.
3. Identify and describe three methods of good land management used by farmers to protect soil resources.
4. Describe the basic steps that make up the water cycle.
5. What is strip mining? Describe the process of land reclamation involved in strip mining.
6. Explain the relationship among overgrazing, erosion, and desertification.

Critical Thinking and Problem Solving

Use the skills you have developed in this chapter to answer each of the following.

1. **Interpreting a chart** The pie chart shows how land that is available to grow crops in the United States is currently being used. What is the total land area available to grow crops? Of that total, how much land is currently being used as farmland? What percentage is that of the total? What other uses are shown on the chart? What percentage of the total available land area do these uses together represent?

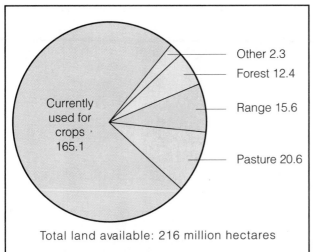

Other 2.3
Forest 12.4
Range 15.6
Currently used for crops 165.1
Pasture 20.6

Total land available: 216 million hectares

2. **Applying concepts** Why is it an advantage for a farmer to use good land-management methods?

3. **Making a graph** From AD 650 to AD 1650 the Earth's population doubled from 250 million to 500 million people. This doubling of the Earth's population took 1000 years. But now the Earth's population doubles about every 33 years. The population of the Earth in 1990 was 5 billion people. Assuming that the growth rate does not change, determine the Earth's population for the years 2023, 2056, and 2089. Graph your results. How much greater will the Earth's population be 100 years from now? Relate this population increase to our use of natural resources.

4. **Developing a model** Plan a "new town" to replace the town you live in. Consider the placement of factories, shopping malls, parks and recreational facilities, housing developments, farms, and roads. Draw a map of your new town and explain why you located each facility where you did.

5. **Using the writing process** A land developer has recently bought a large area of productive farmland near your town. The developer plans to convert the land into a low-rent housing development. Write an article for your local newspaper explaining why you think this use of the land will or will not be good for the town.

Pollution

Guide for Reading

After you read the following sections, you will be able to

3–1 What Is Pollution?
- ■ Define pollution and give some examples of it.

3–2 Land Pollution
- ■ Describe how obtaining and using energy resources can cause land pollution.

3–3 Air Pollution
- ■ Describe how using fossil fuel resources can cause air pollution.

3–4 Water Pollution
- ■ Describe how obtaining and using certain energy resources can cause water pollution.
- ■ Discuss other sources of water pollution.

3–5 What Can Be Done About Pollution?
- ■ Discuss some ways to reduce pollution.

The first sign of danger came with the southeast wind. Instruments at a Swedish nuclear power plant detected twice as much radioactivity in the atmosphere as usual on April 28, 1986. At first the Swedes feared a malfunction in their own power plant. But it soon became apparent that the excess radioactivity was being carried by winds from the Soviet Union.

An explosion and fire at the Chernobyl nuclear power plant in the Ukraine had released a huge cloud of radioactive dust. The cloud was blown by winds across Poland and into Scandinavia. Later the winds shifted and blew the deadly cloud over Switzerland and Italy. Everywhere the cloud was blown, people were warned to avoid contaminated water, vegetables, and milk.

The accident at Chernobyl undoubtedly will have an effect on the further development of nuclear power. Once thought to be the energy source of the future, nuclear power is now viewed with skepticism by many people. Our society could not exist without sources of energy. But, as we must keep in mind, using energy presents certain problems. In this chapter you will learn about some of these problems—their causes and solutions.

Journal *Activity*

You and Your World Have you seen any examples of pollution in your neighborhood? If so, was it litter, smog, polluted water, or some other type of pollution? In your journal, draw a picture of the kind of pollution you observed. Describe the pollution and what you think could be done to prevent it.

◀ *The damage caused by the explosion and fire at the Chernobyl nuclear power plant can be seen in the center of this photograph.*

3-1 What Is Pollution?

Of all the planets in our solar system, only Earth (as far as we know) is home to humans and other living things. Earth provides everything—air, water, food, energy—we need to survive. The environment seems to contain such an abundance of the natural resources needed by humans and other living things that it is hard to imagine ever being without them. Yet that is just what might happen if we are not careful. Despite the richness of Earth's natural resources, a delicate balance between plenty and scarcity exists in our environment.

The balance of the environment can be upset by the way in which humans obtain and use natural resources. If we use renewable resources faster than they can be replaced, the balance will be upset. If we quickly consume nonrenewable resources, which cannot be replaced, the balance will be upset. And if we damage one resource in the process of obtaining or using another resource, the balance will be upset. It is this last problem—the problem of **pollution**—that is the focus of attention in this chapter.

Figure 3-1 *Keeping our environment beautiful is something everyone favors (right). Yet litter discarded by careless people can quickly upset the balance of the environment (left). How can littering be prevented?*

Pollution has become a household word. But what exactly is pollution? Pollution is the release into the environment of substances that change the environment for the worse. Most pollution is the result of human activities. In obtaining and using the natural resources we depend on, we produce pollutants. As one ecologist (a person who studies the relationships among living things and their environment) has written, pollutants are the "normal byproducts of people."

The Trail of Pollution

To better understand the process of pollution, consider a can of soda. To obtain the aluminum to make the can, ore containing aluminum is dug out of the ground. This digging scars the land. Later, in various factory processes, chemicals are used to remove the aluminum from the ore. Any remaining chemicals and impurities are often washed away with water. The waste water is then discarded—and may end up in a river or a stream. The chemicals, so useful in the factory, become pollutants in the water.

Next, the purified aluminum is sent to a manufacturing plant to be turned into a can. Energy is needed to make the can. So a fuel such as coal or oil is burned to provide the energy. As a result of burning fuel, smoke, soot, and gases are released as pollutants into the air. Making the soda that goes into the can also produces land, air, and water pollutants.

Finally, the can of soda may be transported to a supermarket by a truck that burns gasoline and releases air pollutants. But the trail of pollution does not end at the market. Eventually, the can of soda ends up in the hands of a consumer. That person drinks the soda and may then carelessly toss the empty can into the gutter at the side of a road. There it becomes part of an unsightly collection of cans, bottles, plastic bags, old newspapers, and all sorts of other trash. In other words, it becomes litter! This litter is more than an eyesore. It is a danger to wildlife, and it can contribute to the poisoning of our soil and water resources.

FIND OUT BY DOING

A Pollution Survey

Conduct a survey of the area in which you live to determine the extent of land, air, and water pollution. Draw a map of the area. Identify major landmarks, streets, roads, rivers, streams, lakes, and factories. Label the directions north, south, east, and west on the map. Mark any polluted areas and include a key using a different symbol for each type of pollution. Which sections of the area were most polluted? With which types of pollution?

■ What was the cause of pollution in each area you identified?

Figure 3-2 *The trail of pollution leads from waste water discharged into a stream to an overflowing garbage can on a city street.*

Sources and Solutions

As the example of the soda can illustrates, pollution can be thought of as the damage done to one resource by our use of other resources. Although pollution cannot be blamed entirely on our use of energy resources, a great amount of pollution is tied directly to energy use. Our heavy dependence on fossil fuels (coal, oil, and natural gas) has made pollution a major concern in the last several decades. The activities involved in obtaining and using fossil fuels have led to serious land, air, and water pollution.

There is no easy answer to the problem of pollution. Fortunately, there are ways to avoid polluting the environment. Maintaining the balance of the environment does not necessarily mean we must abandon all activities that threaten the balance. Rather, the solution may involve new ways to regulate and reuse materials so that they become new resources. Let's now examine more closely the three main types of pollution—land, air, and water pollution—and the ways in which people are fighting them.

3-1 Section Review

1. How does the use of natural resources by humans affect the environment?
2. What is pollution? What is the cause of most pollution?
3. Describe three ways in which making a can of soda can pollute the environment.

Connection—*Language Arts*
4. The word pollution is derived from a Latin root meaning to soil. The Latin word, in turn, comes from a Greek word meaning dirt. Relate this derivation of the word pollution to the definition of pollution given in this section.

3-2 Land Pollution

In Chapter 1, you learned about many different types of energy resources: fossil fuels, solar energy, wind and water energy, and nuclear energy, as well as various alternative energy resources. Solar, wind, water, and alternative resources together account for only 5 percent of the energy used by people. Most of our energy (about 90 percent) comes from fossil fuels. The remaining 5 percent of the energy we use comes from nuclear power plants. **Obtaining and using certain energy resources—fossil fuels and nuclear energy—can pollute the land.**

The use of coal as a fuel was an important step in the industrialization of the United States. Unfortunately, the environment has often paid heavily for our use of coal. Coal near the surface of the ground is obtained by the process of strip mining. In strip mining, entire hills are torn apart by large earth-moving machines. This process badly damages the land. In addition to scarring the landscape, strip mining also causes land and soil pollution.

During the strip-mining process, fertile topsoil is buried under tons of rock. When the rock is exposed to precipitation (rain, snow, sleet, and hail), acids and other dangerous chemicals may be washed out of the rock by rainwater. The acids and chemicals then seep into the ground, polluting the land and soil.

Hazardous Wastes

Strip mining is just one example of how using energy resources can pollute the land. Another example involves the wastes produced by factories. Wastes from factories may pollute the land with toxic, or poisonous, chemicals. These toxic chemicals are called **hazardous wastes.** Hazardous wastes are any wastes that can cause death or serious damage to human health.

Factories that produce fuels and petrochemicals from petroleum are the major sources of hazardous wastes. When improperly stored in barrels buried in waste dumps, hazardous wastes can seep into the soil and cause land pollution. Cleaning up wastes that were improperly disposed of in the past is a serious problem today.

There are several possible solutions to the management of hazardous wastes. The best way to solve the problem of hazardous wastes, of course, is to produce less of them. In some cases, it might be possible for industry to reuse certain hazardous wastes. Other wastes might be chemically treated to change the toxic substances they contain into nontoxic

Figure 3-3 *When hazardous wastes are not properly disposed of, toxic chemicals may leak into the environment. Cleaning up these wastes is difficult, dangerous, and expensive.*

substances before disposing of them. But chemical treatment of hazardous wastes is usually expensive. Most hazardous wastes wind up buried deep underground, where they are a potential source of land pollution.

Radioactive Wastes

Perhaps the most threatening form of land pollution today involves the disposal of **radioactive wastes.** Radioactive wastes are the wastes produced as a result of the production of energy in nuclear power plants. Radioactive wastes are classified as either high-level or low-level wastes.

High-level wastes are primarily the used fuel rods from a nuclear reactor. Low-level wastes are, by definition, any radioactive wastes that are not high-level wastes. Low-level wastes may include contaminated clothing worn by the power-plant workers or contaminated equipment used in the power plant.

Low-level wastes have relatively short half-lives. The half-life of a radioactive substance is the time it takes for half the substance to decay, or change into a nonradioactive substance. Low-level wastes decay quickly. The disposal of these wastes usually does not cause major land-pollution problems. When properly stored, the wastes can be isolated from the environment until they are no longer radioactive.

High-level wastes, however, may have half-lives of 10,000 years or more. Isolating these wastes from the environment for that length of time is practically impossible. In the past, a common practice was to seal high-level wastes in concrete or glass containers and then bury the containers deep underground. The problem with this procedure is that the containers may eventually corrode or leak, allowing the radioactive wastes to escape and pollute the land.

Recently, several alternative solutions for the disposal of high-level wastes have been suggested. These include geologic disposal, or disposal deep in the Earth. For example, wastes can be buried in rock formations that are not subject to movement or in salt mines. Disposal in deep ocean beds is another alternative. Some scientists have even suggested that it might be possible to shoot rockets carrying high-level wastes into the sun. Finding a way to dispose of

Figure 3–4 *High-level radioactive wastes from nuclear reactors are buried in special containers (top). Some low-level wastes are the result of beneficial nuclear medicine. In Brazil, part of a radiotherapy machine from a clinic was illegally dumped in a junk yard. Several people died after handling the exposed radioactive material. Here you see their lead coffins (bottom). A technician monitors the area for excess radiation.*

high-level radioactive wastes safely is one of the most important environmental issues facing us at this time.

Solid Wastes

Americans produce about 4 billion tons of solid wastes every year. **Solid wastes are useless, unwanted, or discarded materials. They include agricultural wastes, commercial and industrial wastes, and household wastes.** Another word for solid wastes is garbage. The solid wastes found in a garbage dump may include old newspapers and other paper products, glass bottles, aluminum cans, rubber and plastics, discarded food, and yard wastes.

Mountains of garbage in solid-waste dumps once surrounded many cities. Solid-waste dumps are offensive to the eyes as well as to the nose! One way to deal with solid-waste dumps is to cover open dumps with thick layers of soil. In 1976, the United States Congress prohibited open dumps. They ruled that all existing open dumps were to be converted to **sanitary landfills.** In a sanitary landfill, all garbage is compacted, or packed into the smallest possible space. And the garbage is covered at least once a day with a layer of soil. No hazardous wastes are allowed to be dumped in a sanitary landfill. One of the advantages of sanitary landfills is that once they are filled to capacity, they can be landscaped and used as parks, golf courses, and other recreational facilities.

Sanitary landfills can still pose problems, however. Wastes can ooze out of landfills and pollute the surrounding soil. And although sanitary landfills are not supposed to be used for hazardous wastes, household wastes often include pesticides, cleaning materials, paint and paint thinners, and other toxic chemicals.

Another problem with sanitary landfills is that when compacted garbage begins to decompose, or break down, methane gas is produced. Methane gas is dangerous to breathe. It is also a fire hazard. A number of landfill fires have smoldered underground for years, and a few landfills have exploded. This problem can be solved by installing a "gas well" in a landfill. In this way, the methane gas can be removed and used as a fuel.

FIND OUT BY DOING

Garbage Hunt

How much garbage do you usually throw away in a week? To find out, try carrying a garbage bag around with you for a week. Instead of throwing away nonperishable items, such as cans, bottles, newspapers, and so forth, put them in the garbage bag. At the end of the week, you may be surprised at how much you have accumulated!

■ Is there any way in which you could reduce the amount of garbage you throw away?

But the most serious problem with sanitary land-fills may be finding a place to put them. At present, sanitary landfills cannot handle more than a fraction of the solid wastes produced in this country. A city of a million people can produce enough garbage to fill a football stadium in just a year! Most residents probably would not be happy with a landfill nearby. So finding sites to build new sanitary landfills is difficult.

Alternatives to sanitary landfills include ocean dumping, burning, and recycling. At one time, solid wastes were commonly towed offshore and dumped into the ocean. Even today, about 50 million tons of wastes are dumped into the oceans every year. Ocean dumping often results in washed-up debris on beaches, causing more land pollution. But because of the low cost of ocean dumping, many coastal cities consider it an alternative to landfills.

Figure 3–5 *Solid wastes are disposed of in a sanitary landfill (left). Shea Stadium in New York City is one of many recreational facilities around the country built on the site of a sanitary landfill (right).*

Figure 3–6 *Why is ocean dumping of garbage not a good alternative to sanitary landfills?*

Figure 3–7 *Recycling reduces the volume of solid wastes and helps preserve natural resources. How can you make recycling a part of your life?*

Burning garbage in open dumps and in the incinerators of apartment buildings, hospitals, and factories was at one time a popular alternative to landfills. Because burning releases harmful gases, however, this practice is being halted. Sometimes the old incinerators are replaced with highly efficient incinerators fitted with emission controls. But there is another way to burn garbage that is increasingly being used. Since the 1960s, several European countries have used special waste-to-energy incinerators to burn their garbage. The heat produced is used to convert water into steam, which is then used to generate electricity or to heat the buildings. Some of these waste-to-energy incinerators are in use in the United States, and more are planned for the future.

Recycling, which not only gets rid of solid wastes but also creates useful materials, is considered the solid-waste solution of the future by most environmentalists. You will learn more about recycling in Chapter 4. Recycling often involves high technology. Technology alone, however, can do little. People must also be involved. Recycling begins at home. An aluminum can or a glass bottle carelessly tossed to the side of the road can take thousands of years to decompose. Everybody, to a certain degree, causes land pollution. And everybody can help to stop it.

3–2 Section Review

1. Describe two ways in which obtaining and using fossil-fuel resources results in land pollution.
2. What are radioactive wastes? What is the difference between high-level and low-level wastes?
3. What are solid wastes? What are three sources of solid wastes?
4. Describe four methods of solid-waste disposal.

Connection—*You and Your World*
5. For one week, keep a list of all the solid wastes you throw away. What percentage of your solid wastes consists of renewable resources (paper, wood, and so on)? What percentage consists of nonrenewable resources (metals, plastics, and so on)?

The Diaper Dilemma

Disposable paper diapers make up 2 percent of all the garbage produced in this country, adding to the mountains of solid wastes in sanitary landfills. As a result, many parents have chosen reusable cloth diapers instead. But are these reusable diapers really less harmful to the environment than disposable diapers? You decide. The following chart compares resources used and pollutants produced per week by both kinds of diapers.

Based on the risks and benefits associated with their use, which kind of diaper would you choose? Why? What other factors might you consider in making your decision?

	Reusable Diapers	Disposable Diapers
Resources Used		
Renewable	0.18 kilogram	9.72 kilograms
Nonrenewable	1.44 kilogram	1.67 kilograms
Water Used	547 liters	90 liters
Energy Used		
Renewable Sources	14,890 BTU*	3,720 BTU
Nonrenewable Sources	64,000 BTU	19,570 BTU
Pollutants Produced		
Air	0.39 kilogram	0.04 kilogram
Water	0.05 kilograms	0.005 kilogram

*BTU stands for British thermal unit. One BTU is the amount of heat needed to raise the temperature of one pound of water one degree Fahrenheit.

3–3 Air Pollution

When you think of the Earth's natural resources—land, water, minerals, fossil fuels—the one resource that may not come to mind immediately is air. Yet air is probably the most important resource of all. Where would we be without fresh, clean air to breathe? We usually do not think of air as a resource because, although it is all around us, air is normally invisible—odorless, colorless, and tasteless.

But now imagine a place where the sky is always gray, the buildings are blackened by soot, and the air smells like rotten eggs. Do you think people would choose to live in such a place? Would you? The people of Donora, Pennsylvania, did live in such a place in the 1940s.

The city of Donora boasted one of the largest steel mills in the world. The economy of the city was thriving as mills and factories operated 24 hours a day. Millions of tons of coal were burned every hour to provide energy for this growing industrial center. And the people of Donora reasoned that the gray sky, the soot, and the smell were the price they had to pay for progress.

But in October 1948 the price became too high. The air became almost unbreathable. Noontime looked like late evening. People could barely see. They suffered from eye irritations and chest pains. Even the animals became sick. What had happened to this Pennsylvania city in which the autumn air was usually cool and damp? The answer is that on that October day in Donora, a phenomenon known as a **temperature inversion** had settled over the city.

A temperature inversion occurs when cool air near the Earth's surface becomes trapped under a layer of warm air. Normally, cool air is heated by the Earth's surface and rises, taking pollutants with it. But during a temperature inversion, the layer of warmer air acts as a lid, and the pollutants are trapped in the cooler air near the surface. The temperature inversion in Donora, in which 20 people died and thousands more were hospitalized, lasted for four days.

Figure 3–8 *During a temperature inversion, cool air containing pollutants becomes trapped under a layer of warm air. Why is a temperature inversion dangerous to human health?*

Cold, clean air

Warm air

Trapped cool air with pollutants

Since the Donora disaster, cities and states have passed laws to control emissions of pollutants from factories and power plants. Yet the problems associated with burning coal and other fossil fuels still remain. **Although much air pollution comes from the industrial burning of coal and other fossil fuels, the most significant source of air pollution is motor vehicles.** Now let's find out how motor vehicles contribute to air pollution.

Smog

The air that makes up the Earth's atmosphere is a mixture of several gases. These gases include oxygen, nitrogen, carbon dioxide, and water vapor. When fossil fuels are burned, a brew of pollutants enters the air. The gasoline burned in the engines of automobiles and other motor vehicles contains hydrocarbons, or compounds of hydrogen and carbon. Pollution occurs when the gasoline is not completely burned in the engine. Some hydrocarbons escape into the air. At the same time, the poisonous gas carbon monoxide is produced and also enters the air.

Hydrocarbons, carbon monoxide, and several other gases often react in sunlight to form a thick brownish haze called **smog.** (The word smog is a combination of the words smoke and fog.) Smog contains chemicals that irritate the eyes and make

Figure 3–9 *In this photograph, much of Los Angeles is hidden by the smog caused by a temperature inversion. How does automobile exhaust add to the smog problem in Los Angeles?*

FIND OUT BY DOING

How Acid Is Your Rain?

Find out if there is an acid rain problem in your area.

1. The next time it rains, collect a sample of rainwater in a clean glass jar. Label it Sample A.

2. Place some distilled water in another jar and label it Sample B.

3. Obtain some pH paper (used to measure acidity) from your teacher. Your teacher will show you how to use the pH paper to test the acidity of each of your samples. Record your results. Was there a difference in acidity between the two water samples? If so, what might have caused the difference?

breathing difficult. Smog is expecially damaging—even deadly—for people with lung diseases or other respiratory disorders, such as asthma. The pollutants in smog can also damage or kill plants.

Smog can build up over a city because of the flip-flop in layers of air that takes place during a temperature inversion. This is what happened in Donora for four days in 1948. But it happens in Los Angeles all the time. Los Angeles has frequent temperature inversions. As a result, the air in the city is unhealthy for more than 200 days out of the year. In fact, the term smog was invented in Los Angeles.

Acid Rain

Factory smokestacks and automobile exhausts release various pollutants into the air. Some of these pollutants include sulfur and nitrogen compounds called oxides. In the atmosphere, sulfur oxides and nitrogen oxides combine with water vapor through a series of complex chemical reactions. These reactions result in the formation of two of the strongest acids known: sulfuric acid and nitric acid. These acids can fall to the Earth as precipitation in the form of rain, snow, sleet, and even fog. The general term used for precipitation that is more acidic than normal is **acid rain.**

Figure 3–10 *The damage to trees caused by acid rain can be clearly seen in this photograph. What is the source of acid rain?*

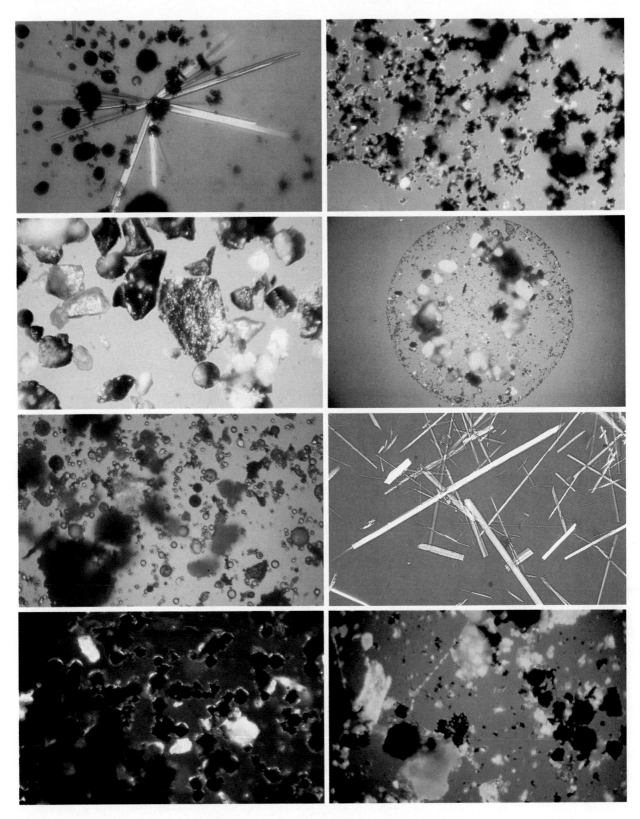

Figure 3–11 *These photographs show some pollutants found in the air. Reading from left to right are sulfate crystals, automobile exhaust, steel mill emissions, a drop of acid rain, coal ash, asbestos particles, oil ash, and emissions from a power plant.*

Very often, acid rain falls many kilometers away from the original source of the pollution. Acid rain from factories in Germany, France, and Great Britain is being blamed for killing fishes and trees in Sweden. Acid rain blown by winds from industrial areas in the midwestern United States is being blamed for damage to lakes and forests in the northeastern United States and in Canada.

The damage caused by acid rain is a serious problem. Naturally, the best way to control acid rain is to stop releasing sulfur and nitrogen oxides into the air. For example, factories could burn coal with a low sulfur content. But low-sulfur coal is expensive and hard to find. So scientists continue to search for additional ways to prevent acid rain and other forms of air pollution.

Indoor Air Pollution

After reading about all the problems caused by air pollution, you may think that the safest place to be is indoors. But think again! Indoor air pollution is an issue that has often been overlooked. Recently, however, scientists have realized that some homes and offices may have serious air-pollution problems.

Several factors combine to make indoor air pollution a serious problem. Some appliances used in homes and offices give off potentially dangerous gases. In addition, many homes and office buildings are well insulated for increased energy efficiency. This means that pollutants that might otherwise escape through cracks and leaks are trapped inside. Also, most people spend more time indoors than they do outdoors.

There are many sources of indoor air pollution. These include the gases given off by wood, coal, and kerosene stoves, as well as the chemicals in air fresheners, disinfectants, and oven and drain cleaners. One of the leading causes of indoor air pollution is smoking. In fact, smoking only one cigarette is the equivalent of breathing the smoggy air of Los Angeles for one to two weeks! Smoking indoors affects nonsmokers as well as smokers. Many communities have recognized the harmful effects of smoking indoors by banning smoking in restaurants, offices, and other public spaces.

Figure 3–12 *Smoking is a leading cause of indoor air pollution. Why is smoking not allowed on public transportation?*

Plants Versus Pollution

Can houseplants reduce indoor air pollution? Dr. W. C. Wolverton thinks they can. Dr. Wolverton has designed a filter system using plants, such as English ivy and peace lilies, that absorb harmful gases and chemicals from the air in homes and offices. But Dr. Wolverton is neither a *florist* nor a *gardener*. He is a former researcher with the National Aeronautics and Space Administration (NASA). In fact, Dr. Wolverton began his research with plants while searching for ways to reduce air pollution on space stations such as *Skylab*. Now he has brought the results of his research down to Earth.

Some scientists are skeptical of Dr. Wolverton's system. They say that the process by which plants absorb air pollutants has still not been determined. Others think that the best way to reduce indoor air pollution is to use materials that do not release pollutants and to improve ventilation. Wolverton, however, is so sure of his results that he has installed a "self-contained bioregeneration system" in his home in Mississippi. In addition, a community college in Mississippi is planning to construct a new math-and-science building using Dr. Wolverton's plant filtration system. This will be the first large-scale test of the system.

If Dr. Wolverton is correct, it may be possible to control indoor air pollution while at the same time adding beauty to our homes and offices. As another researcher has said, even if the system does not work, "having a lot of plants around is nice."

3–3 Section Review

1. What are the major sources of air pollution?
2. What is a temperature inversion? How is it related to air pollution?
3. What is acid rain? How can acid rain cause damage in lakes and forests far from the source of air pollution?
4. What are some sources of indoor air pollution?

Critical Thinking—*Making Inferences*
5. What might be the effect on the economy of an industrial city if strict limitations were placed on the emissions from factories?

3–4 Water Pollution

Water! No living thing—plant, animal, or human—can long survive without this precious liquid. As you have learned in Chapter 2, people use water for drinking, bathing, cooking, and growing crops. Water is also essential for industry and manufacturing. Water is a popular source of recreation, too. As the human population increases, however, agriculture and industry demand more and more water—often more water than is readily available. While some parts of the world have adequate water supplies, other parts of the world are dry.

More and more of the water on the Earth is becoming unusable. One reason for a shortage of usable water is water pollution. **Obtaining and using energy resources are the major causes of water pollution.**

Pollution From Fossil Fuels

In the last section, you read how the emissions from motor vehicles and factories that burn fossil fuels can cause droplets of sulfuric acid and nitric acid to form in the atmosphere. When these droplets fall to the Earth as acid rain, they increase the acidity of lakes, rivers, and streams. Most fishes and

Figure 3–13 *Clean water is one of our most precious natural resources.*

other organisms that live in water can survive in only a narrow range of acidity. By increasing the water's acidity, acid rain kills many of the organisms living in the water. In some parts of the world, entire lakes are now lifeless as a result of acid rain.

Unfortunately, there are other ways in which our energy needs contribute to water pollution. Strip mining for coal releases pollutants that may run off into lakes and streams or may seep into the soil to contaminate groundwater. (Recall from Chapter 2 that half of our drinking-water supply comes from groundwater.)

Our dependence on oil and petroleum products is another source of water pollution. Petroleum is often found under the ocean floor. To obtain this petroleum, offshore oil wells are constructed. Although great precautions are taken during the construction of such wells, drilling accidents do occur. As a result of such accidents, huge amounts of oil spill into the oceans.

Oil spills also occur when tankers carrying oil are damaged, causing their oil to leak into the surrounding water. The first major accident involving an oil tanker took place in 1967, when the tanker *Torrey Canyon* spilled more than 700,000 barrels of oil onto the beaches of England and France. Sadly, there have been many such disasters in the years since—from the *Amoco Cadiz* in 1978 to the *Exxon Valdez* in

Figure 3–14 *During the war in the Persian Gulf, oil was deliberately leaked into the Gulf, creating a huge oil spill (left). Cleaning up a California beach after an oil spill is not an easy task (right).*

1989. It might surprise you to know, however, that more water pollution is caused by the day-to-day operation of oil tankers than by major oil spills. This happens because oil tankers often deliberately flush waste oil directly into the ocean.

Whatever the cause, an oil spill is an environmental disaster. Plants and animals, especially sea birds and aquatic mammals, that come in contact with the oil may be killed. If the oil reaches the shore, it contaminates beaches and may contribute to the death of shore-dwelling organisms. Despite improved cleanup technology, oil spills remain one of the more difficult types of water pollution to remedy.

Pollution From Nuclear Power

Water is needed to cool the reactors in nuclear power plants. Cold water from lakes and rivers is usually used for this purpose. As a result of the cooling process, a large amount of hot water is generated. This heated water is then discharged back into the lakes and rivers. The addition of the heated water causes the temperature of the lakes and rivers to rise. This temperature increase is called **thermal pollution.** Most fishes and other water-dwelling organisms can survive in only a narrow temperature range. When the water temperature rises, many organisms die as a result. In what ways is thermal pollution similar to acid rain?

You read in the last section how radioactive wastes from nuclear power plants can pollute the land. In much the same way, radioactive wastes can become a source of long-term water pollution. Radioactive wastes stored in underground containers may leak out of the containers and pollute groundwater supplies. Pollution of the oceans may result if the containers are dumped at sea.

Hazardous Wastes

Although using and obtaining energy are the major sources of water pollution, they are by no means the only sources. Prior to the 1970s, many industries dumped chemicals and other hazardous wastes directly into streams and other nearby bodies of water. The Cuyahoga River in Cleveland, Ohio,

Figure 3–15 *The cooling towers of a nuclear power plant discharge heated water into a nearby body of water, resulting in thermal pollution. How does thermal pollution affect fishes living in the water?*

was once so polluted with flammable chemical wastes that it caught fire!

Today, chemicals and hazardous wastes are no longer discharged directly into bodies of water. Instead, they are often buried in special landfills. However, even when these wastes are properly contained and buried, it is possible for leaks to occur. Leaks from hazardous-waste landfills may result in groundwater pollution.

Illegal dumping of hazardous wastes is another serious source of groundwater contamination. Containers of hazardous wastes have been dumped illegally in abandoned factories, sanitary landfills, and even vacant lots. This method of illegally disposing of hazardous wastes is called "midnight dumping." Why do you think this name is appropriate for this practice?

Figure 3–16 *Leaking drums of hazardous wastes add to the problem of groundwater pollution.*

Sewage and Agricultural Runoff

Probably the greatest water-pollution threat to human health comes from sewage. Sewage is the waste material that is carried away by sewers and drains. Sewage is sometimes dumped directly into rivers and streams. This sewage often contains disease-causing bacteria and viruses. Drinking water and water used for swimming may become contaminated with these disease-causing organisms. The result is a serious threat to the health of the people who use the contaminated water. Contamination with sewage also makes fishes and other organisms living in the polluted water unfit for human consumption.

Untreated sewage dumped into lakes and rivers is harmful to the fishes and other organisms that live in these bodies of water. Bacteria in the water break down the sewage. In the process, the bacteria use up oxygen. If too much sewage is dumped, too much oxygen is used up. Fishes and other organisms may then die from lack of oxygen.

The runoff of animal wastes and chemicals from farmlands also contributes to water pollution. Chemicals such as phosphates and nitrates are used in fertilizers to improve the growth of crops. When fertilizers run off the land into a lake, they stimulate the growth of algae. The algae then use up the oxygen supply in the lake. Pesticides, which are

FIND OUT BY
DOING

A Sewage-Treatment Plant

Visit a local sewage-treatment plant. Write a report describing how sewage is treated in your community. Be sure to include answers to the following questions:

1. How many stages of treatment does waste water go through before being discharged?

2. Where does your water supply come from?

Figure 3–17 *Waste water must be treated at a sewage-treatment plant to prevent contamination of lakes and rivers (left). Runoff of fertilizers into a pond causes an explosion in the growth of algae (right).*

poisonous chemicals used to kill harmful insects and other pests, can also cause water pollution when they enter lakes and rivers in the runoff from farmlands.

There are a number of ways in which water pollution can be prevented. And scientists are always searching for methods to clean up polluted water. You will learn what can be done to prevent water pollution, as well as land pollution and air pollution, in the section that follows.

FIND OUT BY READING

Silent Spring

In 1962, Rachel Carson published her classic book *Silent Spring,* in which she warned of the dangers of pesticides and other chemicals released into the environment. Read *Silent Spring* and decide if her conclusions still apply today.

3–4 Section Review

1. What are the major sources of water pollution?
2. Describe two ways in which our use of fossil fuels contributes to water pollution.
3. What is thermal pollution? What is the cause of thermal pollution?
4. Describe what happens when fertilizers build up in a lake.

Critical Thinking—*Making Predictions*
5. Predict at least one problem that could result from dumping hazardous wastes into the ocean.

3-5 What Can Be Done About Pollution?

Guide for Reading

Focus on this question as you read.

▶ *What are some ways in which pollution can be reduced?*

Because pollutants are the normal byproducts of human activities, environmental pollution is a problem that will not go away. On the contrary, pollution will get worse as the human population increases. But there are some things that can be done to reduce pollution. **Pollution can be reduced by conserving energy, by finding cleaner ways to use energy, and by making sure that wastes are disposed of in the safest possible ways.** Let's examine some of the ways in which people can help fight pollution.

Conservation

Today, many people are concerned about saving and protecting our natural resources. **Conservation** is the wise use of natural resources so that they will not be used up too quickly or used in a way that will damage the environment. When natural resources are conserved, the environment is benefited in two ways. First, nonrenewable resources last longer. Second, pollution is reduced. Conservation of natural resources will be discussed more fully in Chapter 4.

There are many ways in which energy can be conserved at home. Washing one large load of clothing or dishes instead of several small loads will save energy. Turning down the thermostat on the home heating system a few degrees in the winter and turning up the thermostat on the air conditioner a few degrees in the summer will save energy. And making sure that a house or apartment is well insulated will also save energy.

Because a lot of energy is used by motor vehicles, changing driving habits can make a real difference in the quality of the environment. The use of car pools and public transportation saves fuel and reduces air pollution. So does keeping an automobile well tuned and in good operating condition. Riding a bicycle instead of driving a car for short trips also helps. And don't forget the most ancient (and nonpolluting) form of transportation: walking!

Figure 3-18 *Everyone can learn to use energy wisely. How does home insulation help to conserve energy?*

Figure 3–19 *Reducing pollution does not have to depend on the development of new technologies. If more people rode bicycles or used public transportation, what effect would this have on air pollution?*

A form of conservation that has received considerable public attention is recycling. You probably have a recycling center in your neighborhood or town. Resources that are reclaimed from recycled materials can be sent to factories and used again. Recycling has been successful in reclaiming paper, glass bottles and jars, and aluminum cans.

New Technologies

New technologies can reduce pollution by creating cleaner and more efficient ways of obtaining and using energy resources. Technology can also help develop alternatives to fossil fuels. You have learned about some of these alternative energy sources in Chapter 1. If a clean, renewable source of energy such as solar energy or nuclear fusion could be used on a large scale, many of our current pollution problems would be solved.

The burning of coal has been made less damaging to the environment by the use of scrubber systems. A scrubber system works like a shower. As sulfur oxides are released from burning coal, a high-pressure spray of water dissolves the oxides before they can react with water vapor in the atmosphere. Scrubber systems and other air-pollution-control devices can be used on smokestacks to prevent the release of pollutants into the atmosphere.

Pollution from automobile exhaust has been reduced by equipping cars with pollution-control devices. This type of pollution could be further reduced by the development of engines that burn fuel more completely.

Scientists are exploring new methods of drilling for oil under the ocean floor in order to reduce the possibility of underwater leaks. In addition, several new methods have been developed for cleaning up oil spills. These include vacuum systems that can pump oil out of the water, certain types of absorbent materials that can soak up oil near the shore, and "oil-eating" bacteria that have been developed through genetic-engineering techniques.

FIND OUT BY DOING

Car Pooling

Select a safe spot where you can observe cars as they go by. (Do not choose a busy highway because you will not be able to keep track of every car.) Try to observe the cars at different times each day for several days. For 10 minutes each day, record the number of people in each car that goes by. Make a chart to display your observations.

How many cars have only the driver? At what times of day? How many have one or more passengers?

■ How might the environment benefit from car pooling?

Waste Disposal

Much pollution is caused by industry. Industrial hazardous wastes and other solid wastes are often buried underground in landfills. But if not buried properly, these wastes can leak out of their containers and severely damage the environment.

Of course, the best way to reduce the problem of pollution from hazardous wastes is to reduce the production of these wastes. But there are also several ways to dispose of hazardous wastes safely. First, the hazardous wastes should be separated from other industrial wastes. Second, as much of the wastes as possible should be reused or recycled. Third, the wastes should be chemically treated to destroy the toxic materials they contain. Finally, the wastes should be buried in secure landfills with many safeguards to prevent leaks into the environment.

Figure 3–20 *The message in this environmental demonstration is "Recycle the trash monster!"*

Everyone's Responsibility

At the beginning of this chapter, you read that pollution is caused mainly by the activities of people. It is important to realize that the activities of people can also reduce pollution. And everyone—young and old, scientist and nonscientist—can help. Remember that in the future you will be responsible for making decisions about ways to reduce pollution. Now is the time to begin. What can you do to help reduce pollution?

3–5 Section Review

1. How can pollution be reduced?
2. What is conservation? How does conservation reduce pollution and protect resources?
3. How can new technologies reduce pollution?
4. List four steps involved in the safe disposal of hazardous wastes.

Connection—*You and Your World*
5. What pollution problems do you think you will face in the next five to ten years? What will you do to solve these problems?

FIND OUT BY

THINKING

Pro or Con?

Write a brief essay that either supports or refutes the following statement: "I think this whole environmental thing has gone too far. If industrial profits go down because of all these government regulations, the country will be worse off than ever."

Laboratory Investigation

Observing Air Pollutants

Problem
How can you observe solid particles in the air that cause air pollution?

Materials

6 petri dishes
petri dish cover
petroleum jelly
glass-marking pencil
graph paper
magnifying glass

Procedure 🔺

1. Coat the flat surface of each petri dish with a thin layer of petroleum jelly.

2. Immediately place the cover on one of the petri dishes. Put the covered dish aside.

3. Place the other five petri dishes in different locations outdoors where they will not be disturbed.

4. Use the glass-marking pencil to write the name of the location on the side of each dish.

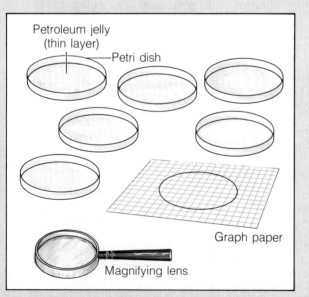

Petroleum jelly (thin layer)
Petri dish
Graph paper
Magnifying lens

5. Leave the dishes undisturbed for 3 days.

6. After 3 days, collect the dishes. Place each dish, one at a time, on the graph paper. Use the magnifying glass to count the number of particles in each square of the graph-paper grid. Calculate the total number of particles in each dish. Record your observations in a data table similar to the one shown here.

Observations

1. Compare the data from each location.

2. Compare the covered dish with the five dishes you placed outdoors.

3. Compare your data with data from other groups. Record the locations of the dishes from the other groups and the number of particles counted in each dish.

Dish	Location	Number of Particles
1		
2		

Analysis and Conclusions

1. Which dish was the control in this investigation? Explain your answer.

2. The solid particles you counted are evidence of air pollution. How can you account for the difference in the number of particles at the various locations?

3. How can you account for the difference in the number of particles found in other locations by your classmates?

4. **On Your Own** Make a bar graph of your data, plotting location on the horizontal axis and number of particles counted on the vertical axis. What conclusions can you draw from your graph?

Study Guide

Summarizing Key Concepts

3–1 What Is Pollution?

▲ The balance of the environment can be upset by the way in which humans obtain and use natural resources.

▲ Pollution is the release into the environment of substances that change the environment for the worse.

▲ The three main types of pollution are land pollution, air pollution, and water pollution.

3–2 Land Pollution

▲ Obtaining and using fossil fuels and nuclear energy can cause land pollution.

▲ Other sources of land pollution are hazardous wastes, radioactive wastes, and solid wastes.

▲ Solid wastes include agricultural wastes, commercial and industrial wastes, and household wastes.

3–3 Air Pollution

▲ The major sources of air pollution are motor vehicles and the burning of coal and other fossil fuels by industry.

▲ Acid rain is caused when sulfur and nitrogen oxides released by burning fossil fuels combine with water vapor in the air to form sulfuric acid and nitric acid.

▲ Indoor air pollution is a serious problem that is often overlooked.

3–4 Water Pollution

▲ Obtaining and using energy resources, especially fossil fuels and nuclear energy, are the major causes of water pollution.

▲ Other sources of water pollution are industrial hazardous wastes, sewage, and agricultural runoff.

3–5 What Can Be Done About Pollution?

▲ Pollution can be reduced by conserving energy, by finding cleaner ways to use energy, and by disposing of wastes in the safest possible ways.

Reviewing Key Terms

Define each term in a complete sentence.

3–1 What Is Pollution?
pollution

3–2 Land Pollution
hazardous waste
radioactive waste
sanitary landfill

3–3 Air Pollution
temperature inversion
smog
acid rain

3–4 Water Pollution
thermal pollution

3–5 What Can Be Done About Pollution?
conservation

Chapter Review

Content Review

Multiple Choice

Choose the letter of the answer that best completes each statement.

1. The major source of air pollution is
   a. hazardous wastes.
   b. radioactive wastes.
   c. burning coal.
   d. motor vehicles.
2. The damage done to one natural resource in the process of using another resource is called
   a. ecology.   c. conservation.
   b. pollution.   d. recycling.
3. Which of the following is an example of hazardous wastes?
   a. toxic chemicals
   b. plastics
   c. yard wastes
   d. old newspapers
4. High-level radioactive wastes are difficult to dispose of because they
   a. take up too much space.
   b. have long half-lives.
   c. are poisonous.
   d. have short half-lives.

5. Pollution can be reduced by
   a. conserving energy.
   b. finding clean ways to use energy.
   c. disposing of wastes safely.
   d. all of these
6. The release of excess heat into nearby bodies of water results in
   a. thermal pollution.
   b. acid rain.
   c. hazardous waste pollution.
   d. groundwater pollution.
7. The term midnight dumping refers to the illegal disposal of
   a. yard wastes.
   b. solid wastes.
   c. hazardous wastes.
   d. untreated sewage.
8. A temperature inversion occurs when
   a. winds are calm.
   b. warm air is trapped under cool air.
   c. cool air is trapped under warm air.
   d. warm air rises.

True or False

If the statement is true, write "true." If it is false, change the underlined word or words to make the statement true.

1. Acid rain is formed when oxides of sulfur and nitrogen combine with <u>oxygen</u> in the air.
2. The wise and careful use of natural resources is called <u>recycling</u>.
3. The wastes produced by nuclear power plants are <u>agricultural</u> wastes.
4. Sanitary landfills are used to dispose of <u>solid</u> wastes.
5. Indoor air pollution <u>is not</u> a serious problem.
6. Growth of algae results from the runoff of <u>fertilizers</u> into a lake.

Concept Mapping

Complete the following concept map for Section 3–1. Refer to pages L6–L7 to construct a concept map for the entire chapter.

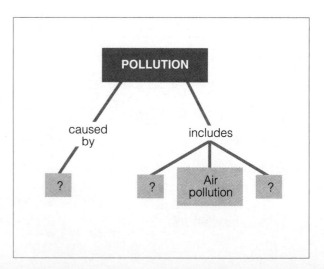

Concept Mastery

Discuss each of the following in a brief paragraph.

1. Explain how the balance of the environment is related to obtaining and using energy resources.
2. What is the relationship between conservation and pollution?
3. Explain why land, air, and water pollution cannot really be separated from one another.
4. Describe the trail of pollution involved in manufacturing a can of soda.
5. What is the most serious problem involved with the use of sanitary landfills? What are three alternatives to the use of sanitary landfills?
6. Describe the chain of events that led to the air-pollution disaster in Donora, Pennsylvania, in October 1948.
7. Why is smog a serious problem in Los Angeles?
8. What is the difference between high-level and low-level radioactive wastes?
9. One serious form of land pollution is solid waste: garbage and litter. Instead of being buried in sanitary landfills, garbage and litter can be burned. Why is burning garbage and litter not an environmentally sound idea? How could it become an environmentally sound idea?

Critical Thinking and Problem Solving

Use the skills you have developed in this chapter to answer each of the following.

1. **Making predictions** Imagine that the year is now 2010. Air pollution has become so bad that Congress has passed a law forbidding the use of private automobiles. How do you think your life might be changed by this law?
2. **Interpreting photographs** Describe the situation shown in this photograph and explain what caused it.

3. **Applying concepts** Pollutants can be thought of as resources in the wrong place. Make a list of some of the pollutants discussed in this chapter. How could they be useful if they were in the right place?
4. **Relating concepts** Discuss how each of the following groups might react to the problem of acid rain in a certain area.
   a. tourists
   b. factory owners
   c. wildlife conservationists
   d. campers on a fishing trip
5. **Using the writing process** Write a short science fiction story describing what you think life will be like in the year 2061. The focus of your story should be the kinds of energy resources used and the environmental problems that may exist.

Conserving Earth's Resources

It was a typically peaceful early morning near the remote town of Valdez on Alaska's southern coast. Then suddenly, at 12:27 AM, came the emergency call from the huge oil tanker *Exxon Valdez:* "I've run aground and we've lost 150,000 barrels." And so began the worst oil-spill disaster on record in the United States.

On March 24, 1989, the *Exxon Valdez* struck Bligh Reef in Prince William Sound. The reef ruptured the hull of the ship, eventually releasing more than 240,000 barrels of crude oil into the water. As the oil slick began to grow, environmentalists, state officials, and experts from Exxon and the federal government tried to develop a plan to clean up the oil as quickly as possible. Their response, however, was too slow to stop the oil from spreading onto the beaches. Despite massive cleanup efforts, it will be many years before the damage to the environment can be corrected.

The Earth's natural resources, such as oil, can cause great harm to the Earth and its inhabitants when used carelessly. They can also be of great value to people when used wisely. In the following pages, you will learn how people can help to protect the environment by the wise use of natural resources.

Journal *Activity*

You and Your World What do you think is meant by the wise use of natural resources? In your journal, draw a picture showing ways in which you, your family, and your community can use resources wisely.

◄ *The oil spill caused by the* Exxon Valdez *(the larger of the two ships in the photograph) resulted in great harm to wildlife in and around Prince William Sound.*

4–1 Fossil Fuels and Minerals

You use natural resources every day of your life. Some of these resources are fossil fuels: coal, oil, and natural gas. Others are minerals, such as aluminum, copper, and iron. Recall from Chapter 2 that fossil fuels and minerals are classified as nonrenewable resources. This means that once they are used up, they cannot be replaced. Because society relies so heavily on nonrenewable resources, conservation of these resources is extremely important. As you learned in Chapter 3, conservation is the wise use of natural resources so that they will not be used up too quickly or used in a way that will damage the environment. **Fossil fuels and minerals can be conserved by saving energy and by recycling.** Let's examine these methods of conservation more closely.

Energy Conservation

The year is 1973. A sea of automobiles stretches for several kilometers. As the sun peeks over the horizon, some motorists read the morning newspapers or try to sleep. The more sociable drivers use the opportunity to chat with their neighbors. The rest just sit in their cars and scowl.

Figure 4–1 *During the gas shortage of 1973, motorists in Connecticut—and elsewhere—had to wait in long lines to buy gasoline. Do you think such shortages could happen again?*

Is this the scene of an early-morning traffic jam? No, it represents the first experience Americans had with an oil shortage. At that time, shipments of oil to the United States were drastically reduced. Motorists had to wait in long lines at gas stations for what had become a most precious resource: gasoline.

Fortunately, the oil crisis of 1973 did not last long. The discovery of new oil fields combined with serious conservation efforts produced a relative abundance of oil by 1986. But the oil shortages of the 1970s remain dramatic illustrations of how dependent people are on fossil fuels and how dangerously close we are to running out of them.

Could the events of 1973 be repeated in the future? Unfortunately, the answer is yes. Modern society relies on fossil fuels for transportation, for industry, for heating and cooling buildings, and for generating electricity. But supplies of fossil fuels are dwindling. Sooner or later, we will run out of them. The goal of energy conservation is to make existing supplies last as long as possible.

How can you help to conserve energy? Here is a list of ways in which you can conserve energy in the home:

- Replace burned-out light bulbs with new energy-efficient bulbs.
- Turn off lights when they are not needed.
- Turn off the television when you are not watching it.

FIND OUT BY DOING

Current Events

Start a scrapbook of current news items concerning environmental problems. Bring your scrapbook to class and organize a class discussion around one or more of the news items. Are the problems worldwide or are they limited to certain parts of the world? How might these events affect you and your classmates? How might they affect living things in the environment?

■ What solutions can you suggest for some of these problems?

Figure 4–2 *By saving energy and using energy efficiently, we may be able to make our natural resources last longer. Why does thawing frozen food before cooking help save energy?*

- Take a quick shower instead of filling the tub for a bath.
- Fix leaking water faucets and pipes.
- Use the clothes washer and dryer only for full loads.
- Use the dishwasher only for full loads or do dishes by hand.
- Allow dishes to air dry instead of using the dry cycle on the dishwasher.
- Thaw frozen foods before putting them in the oven.
- Cook the entire meal in the oven instead of using several burners on the stove.
- Make sure refrigerators and freezers are properly sealed.
- Defrost refrigerators before the ice becomes too thick.
- Set the thermostat on the home heating system as low as possible.

What other ways can you think of to conserve energy in the home?

Energy Efficiency

Another way to conserve fossil fuels is to use them more efficiently. More efficient car engines use less gasoline. Smaller, less massive cars also use less gasoline than larger, more massive cars do. Adding 100 kilograms to the mass of a car increases its consumption of gasoline by 6 percent. Driving slowly also saves gasoline, as well as lives. But the best way to save energy is to leave the car at home and use public transportation: buses, passenger trains, and subways. Most forms of public transportation are at least twice as energy efficient as cars. Riding a bicycle or walking are also energy-saving alternatives.

Recycling

The problem with minerals is similar to the problem with fossil fuels. Once minerals are used up, they are gone forever. One solution to this problem is to find other materials to take the place of minerals. For example, large amounts of steel are used in car engines. Steel is an alloy of iron and several

Figure 4–3 *In Portland, Oregon, many commuters use a new light rail service instead of driving their cars to work. How does such public transportation save energy and also cut down on pollution?*

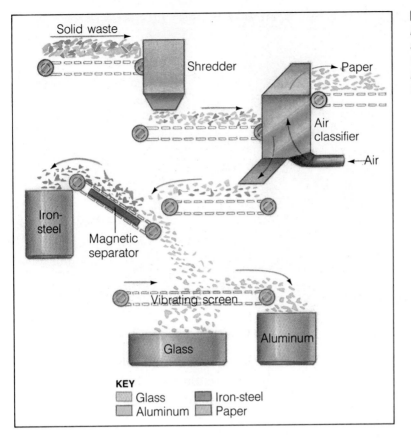

Figure 4-4 *This diagram shows how solid wastes can be separated for recycling. Separating wastes in this way is expensive. Does the value of recycling justify the cost of separation?*

other metals, including chromium and nickel. (Recall that an alloy is a substance made of two or more metals.) Today, scientists are working to replace some parts of these metal engines with plastic parts. If plastics and other materials can replace some minerals, supplies of these minerals will last longer.

Another solution is to keep minerals in usable form by **recycling** them. If recycling became an accepted part of everyday life, existing mineral resources would last longer, less land would be dug up and destroyed in the search for new mineral resources, and the solid-waste problem would be reduced. Recycling also contributes to energy conservation. Making aluminum from recycled cans, for example, uses much less energy than making aluminum from ore.

Although community recycling of solid wastes has become increasingly common, most industries still do not recycle on a large scale. The reason for this is primarily an economic one. Separating solid wastes for recycling is expensive. And even if the separation is done, there is little consumer demand for recycled

Figure 4–5 *Many tons of paper are being recycled at this recycling center. Recycling helps save trees, from which paper is made. Writing paper and envelopes made from maps are some of the products made from recycled paper that are now available to consumers. What other recycled products are you familiar with?*

products. This situation may be changing, however. For example, cellulose insulation made from recycled paper fibers is now competitive with other types of home insulation, such as fiberglass. Finally, when the cost of solid-waste disposal and of the pollution involved is compared with the cost of recycling, recycling can be seen as an economical alternative to disposal.

4–1 Section Review

1. What are two ways to conserve fossil fuels and minerals?
2. What is the goal of energy conservation? List at least four ways to conserve energy in the home.
3. How can automobiles be made to use gasoline more efficiently?
4. Why is recycling not practiced on a large scale by most industries? What can be done to change this?

Critical Thinking—*Relating Concepts*
5. Using plastics instead of steel in car engines is one way to conserve minerals. However, the use of plastics presents other problems. What are some of these problems?

Helping the Victims of an Oil Spill

You have been reading about Earth's nonliving resources and what can be done to protect them. Earth has living resources as well. Among these living resources are the thousands of sea birds and other *wildlife* that may be injured or killed as the result of an oil spill. What can be done to protect these living resources?

In 1988, a relatively "small" oil spill off the coast of Washington State resulted in the deaths of tens of thousands of sea birds. Fortunately, about 4000 birds survived long enough to struggle onto the beaches. When the oil-soaked birds reached shore, volunteers were waiting to transport them to emergency treatment centers. Here the volunteers slowly and carefully washed and dried the birds, trying to remove all traces of oil from their feathers. The volunteers had to treat the birds gently to avoid damaging the feathers. Each bird required at least an hour to bathe and rinse thoroughly.

In spite of all the care they received, fewer than 1000 birds survived to be released back into the environment. And there was no way to know for sure if these birds were able to survive on their own after being released. Even with modern technology and good intentions, humans cannot duplicate an animal's natural survival equipment. Yet they can easily destroy it with just one careless act.

4–2 Protecting the Environment

If nothing is done to prevent pollution, the problem will only get worse as the human population increases. As you learned in Chapter 3, pollution is the release into the environment of substances that change the environment for the worse. Although pollution can be classified as land, air, and water pollution, it is important to remember that all parts of the environment are interrelated. Anything that damages one part of the environment can also damage other parts. Acid rain, for example, begins as air

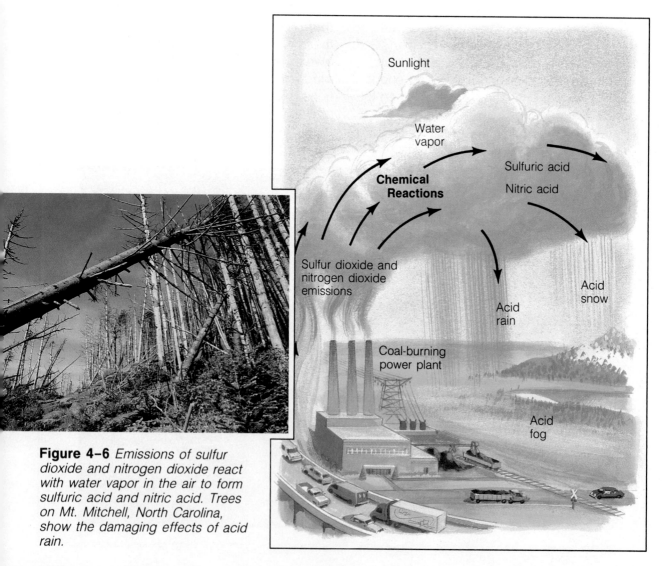

Figure 4–6 *Emissions of sulfur dioxide and nitrogen dioxide react with water vapor in the air to form sulfuric acid and nitric acid. Trees on Mt. Mitchell, North Carolina, show the damaging effects of acid rain.*

pollution. As acid rain falls into lakes and rivers, the problem becomes water pollution. Then as acid rain seeps into the soil, land pollution results. In this example of a "pollution chain," all aspects of the environment are damaged.

What can be done to prevent pollution? There is no easy answer to this question; no single solution to the problem. But there are some actions that can be taken now—before it is too late. **People can help prevent pollution by using energy wisely and by discarding wastes safely.** In the previous section you learned about ways to use energy wisely and efficiently. In the following pages you will read about some specific examples of what can be done to prevent pollution of the environment.

Safeguarding the Air

Gases and particles given off when fossil fuels are burned are called **emissions** (ee-MIHSH-uhnz). In theory, if the burning of fossil fuels such as coal, oil, and natural gas is complete—that is, with enough oxygen present—the only waste products should be carbon dioxide and water vapor. In practice, however, some pollution-causing emissions are always given off as well. These emissions include the poisonous gas carbon monoxide as well as nitrogen oxides

FIND OUT BY
WRITING

The Greenhouse Effect

The carbon dioxide released into the air by motor vehicles and the burning of fossil fuels by industry contributes to the greenhouse effect. Using reference books in the library, write a report on the greenhouse effect. In your report, explain how carbon dioxide increases the greenhouse effect. Also include a discussion of how scientists think the greenhouse effect may change the Earth's climate, as well as the results of such changes.

Figure 4–7 *Emissions released into the air from factory smokestacks cause acid rain and other forms of air pollution. Scrubbers are pollution-control devices that reduce emissions from factory smokestacks.*

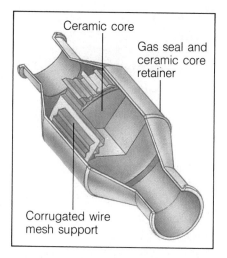

Ceramic core

Gas seal and ceramic core retainer

Corrugated wire mesh support

Figure 4-8 *Automobiles manufactured today are required to have catalytic converters. How does a catalytic converter work?*

FIND OUT BY DOING

Natural Pollution

Pollution is caused by people. But sometimes nature may cause pollution too. Using reference books in the library, look up information about the eruption of the volcano on the island of Krakatoa, which took place in 1883. Write a short report about the effect of this eruption on the Earth's weather in the years that followed. Then compare the Krakatoa eruption with the eruption of Mt. Pinatubo in the Philippines in 1991. Prepare a poster or diorama to illustrate your report.

and sulfur oxides, which cause acid rain when they react with water vapor in the air. But the pollution-causing emissions can be reduced in various ways.

Devices called scrubbers frequently are used to wash suspended particles and sulfur oxides out of smokestack fumes. In some scrubbers, the fumes are passed through a blanket of steam. In the process, most of the pollution-causing emissions are dissolved in the steam. Then as the steam cools, the dissolved waste products rain down into a special collector and are removed. Another kind of scrubber uses a spray of liquid chemicals instead of steam. In this kind of scrubber, sulfur oxides react with the chemical spray to form a solid "sludge" that is then removed.

Emissions from motor vehicles, which are the main sources of air pollution, can be reduced by the use of **catalytic converters.** A catalytic converter is an emission-control device that changes the hydrocarbons and carbon monoxide in automobile exhaust into carbon dioxide and water vapor.

Scrubbers and catalytic converters are only two of the ways scientific technology is helping to clean up the air. In many ways, the air today is much cleaner than it was 10 or 20 years ago. But in some ways, it is more polluted. Environmentalists say that some pollution laws, such as the Clean Air Act of 1970, must be tightened if we are to ensure clean air in the future. The Clean Air Act set up emission standards, which limit the amount of pollutants that can be released into the air from a particular source. And emission-control technology must be improved. In addition, alternative sources of cleaner energy, such as gasohol and hydrogen, must be further developed.

Alternative sources of energy will never eliminate all possible sources of air pollution. And devices to clean emissions will be of little value if they are not used. So it is vital that industry and other sources of air pollution make every effort to meet air-pollution standards set by the government. Furthermore, much air pollution can be traced directly to people. People, for example, drive the cars that add to air pollution. So people should make sure that their cars are well tuned and that the engines and exhaust systems are in good working order.

Figure 4-9 *To eliminate the huge number of cars entering Yosemite National Park every year, the National Park Service hopes to build a solar train to carry visitors through the park. Nonpolluting solar-powered trucks are already being used in Natural Bridges National Monument in Utah.*

Safeguarding Our Water Supplies

In 1972 and 1974, the United States Congress passed two strict laws to fight water pollution. They were the Clean Water Act of 1972 and the Safe Drinking Water Act of 1974. Both these laws were intended to stop the flow of untreated wastes into waterways from **point sources.** Point sources include sewers, pipes, and channels through which wastes are discharged.

These laws set up rules to greatly reduce water pollution from point sources. Towns and cities were required to build sewage-treatment plants or to improve existing plants. Such plants clean wastewater before it is discharged into waterways. Similar treatment plants purify water for drinking. Industries also were required to clean their wastewater before releasing it into lakes, streams, and rivers. Most of these actions were successful. Water quality improved.

The 1972 and 1974 laws greatly reduced water pollution from point sources. The laws did nothing,

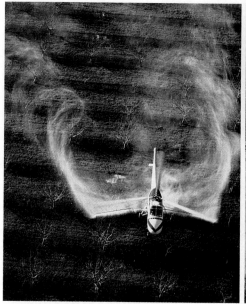

Figure 4-10 *Although it may look as if raw sewage is being dumped into a nearby river, the sewage has actually been treated at a sewage-treatment plant before being discharged. Nonpoint sources of pollution include pesticides sprayed on crops, which end up in our water supplies.*

FIND OUT BY READING

Save the Earth

For an interesting perspective on protecting the environment, read *This Bright Land: A Personal View* by the American journalist and drama critic Brooks Atkinson (1894–1984). Then, to find out what you can do to help, read *Save the Earth: An Ecology Handbook for Kids* by Laurence Pringle.

however, to reduce pollution from **nonpoint sources.** Nonpoint sources of water pollution include sanitary landfills that ooze poisonous liquids and industrial waste ponds that leak into the surrounding ground. Nonpoint sources also include illegally dumped hazardous wastes and runoff of pesticides and fertilizers from various sources.

Unfortunately, the wastes from nonpoint sources are usually the most harmful to the environment. And they are often difficult to find and clean up. For example, drums of hazardous wastes may lie in solid-waste dumps for many years. Often, the drums are not identified as containing hazardous wastes. The drums may even be buried with ordinary garbage in sanitary landfills. When the drums decay, hazardous wastes may leak into the soil and groundwater. The drums may be uncovered years later, causing a nightmare for the people who must clean up the damage—if it can indeed be cleaned up.

What is the solution? Obviously, hazardous waste dumps must be checked carefully for leakage. Whenever possible, hazardous wastes should be disposed of properly at the factory or manufacturing plant where they are produced. Such disposal can be difficult and expensive. But proper disposal is far less difficult and costly than removing these hazardous wastes from the environment years later.

PROBLEM Solving

People Are Part of the Environment Too

Environmental problems cannot be viewed only as scientific problems. Because they involve people and the way people live, they must be viewed as economic, social, and political problems as well. Consider, for example, the following situation:

The city of Pleasant Grove centers around a large factory that makes machine parts. About half the families in Pleasant Grove have at least one family member working at the factory. The factory contributes significantly to air and water pollution through smokestack emissions and large amounts of chemical wastes. The factory manager recently announced that the factory will increase operations by 35 percent during the next year. The expansion will include the addition of a night shift and the purchase of a wooded area next to the factory. This land will be used for additional manufacturing facilities and for a second parking lot.

Imagine that you are a magazine reporter who has been sent to Pleasant Grove. Your assignment is to find out how the following people feel about the planned expansion of the factory: a scientist; a conservationist; an economist; an average citizen; a local politician. Write a magazine article describing the reactions of each person.

4–2 Section Review

1. How can people help prevent pollution of the environment?
2. Use the example of acid rain to describe how pollution affects all parts of the environment.
3. How do scrubbers and catalytic converters reduce harmful emissions from smokestacks and automobiles?
4. What is the difference between point sources and nonpoint sources of pollution?

Connection—*You and Your World*
5. In what ways can you personally help reduce pollution?

Laboratory Investigation

Comparing the Decomposition of Different Types of Litter in a Landfill

Problem

Large amounts of litter and garbage are buried in sanitary landfills every day. How fast do different materials decompose in a model landfill?

Materials *(per group)*

4-L glass jar with lid
topsoil
litter (orange peels, paper, scrap metal, and so forth)
glass-marking pencil

Procedure 🔺

1. Cover the bottom of the glass jar with a layer of soil.
2. Place one third of the litter in the jar. Make sure the litter is near the sides of the jar so you can see it.
3. With the glass-marking pencil, circle the location of each item of litter on the outside of the jar.

4. Add another layer of soil on top of the litter.
5. Place another one third of the litter in the jar. Mark the location of each item of litter with the glass-marking pencil.
6. Add another layer of soil on top of the litter.
7. Place the last of the litter in the jar. Mark the location of each item of litter.
8. Cover the litter with a final layer of soil. Add water to the jar until all the soil is slightly moist. Put the lid on the jar.
9. Observe your model landfill once a week for a month. Predict whether or not each item of litter will decompose.

Observations

1. Describe the appearance of each item of litter in the jar after one day, one week, two weeks, and one month. Record your observations in a data table.
2. Which items of litter decomposed fastest? Which items decomposed more slowly? Which items did not decompose at all?

Analysis and Conclusions

1. Compare the kinds of litter and their decomposition rates. Were your predictions correct? Is there any pattern to the litter that decomposed as compared with the litter that did not decompose?
2. Based on your observations, what recommendations would you make to a town that was planning to build a sanitary landfill?
3. **On Your Own**   Suppose the soil, jar, water, and litter had been sterilized before the investigation. Would the results have been the same? Explain. Design an experiment to test your conclusion.

Summarizing Key Concepts

4–1 Fossil Fuels and Minerals

▲ Fossil fuels and minerals are classified as nonrenewable resources.

▲ Conservation is the wise use of natural resources so that they will not be used up too quickly or used in a way that will damage the environment.

▲ Fossil fuels and minerals can be conserved by saving energy and by recycling.

▲ The goal of energy conservation is to make existing supplies of fossil fuels last as long as possible.

▲ There are many ways in which you can conserve energy in your home—from turning off lights to lowering the thermostat.

▲ Two ways to make mineral resources last longer are to use other materials in place of minerals and to keep minerals in usable form by recycling.

4–2 Protecting the Environment

▲ Although pollution can be classified as land, air, and water pollution, all parts of the environment are interrelated, and thus pollution of one part often affects the others.

▲ Pollution can be prevented by using energy wisely and by discarding wastes safely.

▲ Emissions are gases and particles given off when fossil fuels are burned.

▲ Emissions from smokestacks can be removed by scrubbers.

▲ Emissions from motor vehicles can be removed by catalytic converters.

▲ Laws have been passed to reduce water pollution from point sources, such as sewers.

▲ Pollution from nonpoint sources, such as hazardous wastes and agricultural runoff, is especially harmful to the environment.

Reviewing Key Terms

Define each term in a complete sentence.

4–1 Fossil Fuels and Minerals
recycling

4–2 Protecting the Environment
emission.
catalytic converter
point source
nonpoint source

Chapter Review

Multiple Choice

Choose the letter of the answer that best completes each statement.

1. Using resources wisely is called
   a. ecology.
   b. conservation.
   c. pollution.
   d. waste disposal.
2. A catalytic converter changes pollution-causing emissions in automobile exhaust into carbon dioxide and
   a. carbon monoxide.
   b. water vapor.
   c. hydrocarbons.
   d. sulfur dioxide.
3. Automobiles can be made to burn fuel more efficiently by
   a. making them larger.
   b. driving faster.
   c. driving slower.
   d. increasing their mass.
4. Recycling is not done by most industries because it
   a. is too expensive.
   b. requires too much energy.
   c. is cheaper to use plastics.
   d. is too time consuming.

5. Emissions from factory smokestacks can be reduced through the use of
   a. catalytic converters.
   b. high-sulfur coal.
   c. scrubbers.
   d. all of these
6. Acid rain is a serious form of
   a. air pollution.
   b. water pollution.
   c. land pollution.
   d. all of these
7. Energy can be conserved by
   a. fixing leaky faucets.
   b. taking showers instead of baths.
   c. lowering the thermostat.
   d. all of these
8. Aluminum and copper are examples of
   a. fossil fuels.
   b. pollutants.
   c. minerals.
   d. emissions.
9. Point sources of pollution include
   a. sewers.
   b. hazardous wastes.
   c. agricultural runoff.
   d. sanitary landfills.

True or False

If the statement is true, write "true." If it is false, change the underlined word or words to make the statement true.

1. Fossil fuels and minerals are <u>renewable</u> resources.
2. Automobiles are <u>more</u> energy efficient than most forms of public transportation.
3. Making aluminum from ore requires <u>less</u> energy than making aluminum from recycled cans.
4. As the human population increases, the problem of pollution will <u>decrease</u>.
5. Two kinds of emission-control devices are scrubbers and <u>catalytic converters</u>.
6. Sewers are examples of <u>nonpoint</u> sources of water pollution.
7. Pollution of one part of the environment <u>cannot</u> affect other parts.

Concept Mapping

Complete the following concept map for Section 4–1. Refer to pages L6–L7 to construct a concept map for the entire chapter.

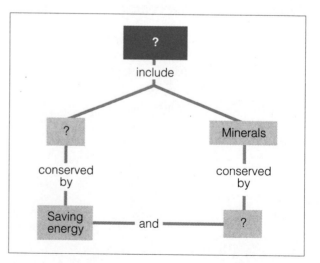

Concept Mastery

Discuss each of the following in a brief paragraph.

1. What are some ways to conserve energy in the home?
2. Why is the conservation of fossil fuels important?
3. What was the purpose of the Clean Water Act and the Safe Drinking Water Act?
4. What are some benefits of recycling?
5. What are emissions? How can pollution-causing emissions be reduced?
6. What are two ways to conserve mineral resources?
7. Why is pollution from nonpoint sources a more serious threat to the environment than pollution from point sources?

Critical Thinking and Problem Solving

Use the skills you have developed in this chapter to answer each of the following.

1. **Relating concepts** How does recycling contribute to energy conservation?
2. **Interpreting a photograph** Does the photograph show a point source or a nonpoint source of pollution? How can you tell?

3. **Applying concepts** Explain how each of the following helps to conserve energy:
   a. Turning off the TV when no one is watching it
   b. Defrosting the refrigerator
   c. Driving an energy-efficient car
   d. Taking a shower instead of a bath
4. **Making diagrams** Draw a chart or diagram that shows a pollution chain in which emissions from burning fossil fuels or fumes from toxic chemicals begin as air pollutants and then become water pollutants and land pollutants.
5. **Relating cause and effect** Identify a possible cause for each of the following:
   a. Most farmers stop using pesticides.
   b. The United States runs out of oil.
   c. Industries routinely recycle materials.
   d. More and more people use public transportation.
6. **Using the writing process** Write a brief essay in which you express your opinion about the following statement: "These gloomy predictions about running out of oil are greatly exaggerated. And even if we do run out, I feel confident that humans, with all their resourcefulness, will find another way to produce the energy they need."

GAZETTE

DR. MBAYMA ATALIA

PHOTO: RAYMOND BONNER/NEW YORK TIME8 PICTURE8

Keeping the White Rhino Alive

Taking care not to let the animal catch his scent, the researcher crouches down in the tall grass and begins to take notes. The object of his attention is a white rhinoceros—a bulky grayish mammal with a pointed horn and a large square mouth. Quickly, the researcher notes the time of day, what the rhino is eating, its geographical location, and how far it has moved since last seen. Meanwhile, the rhino continues to graze like a vacuum cleaner, eating everything in sight. After about 20 minutes of intense eating, the temporarily satisfied rhino moves off at a half trot in search of its next meal.

Constant eating is a well-established habit of the white rhino, the world's second largest land mammal. Few people know the habits of this great creature better than Dr. Mbayma Atalia, a researcher and protection officer at Garamba National Park in Zaire, Africa. Dr. Mbayma has spent years studying the sleeping and grazing patterns of the white rhino. He knows his subjects so well that he can recognize every rhinoceros in the park simply by the shape of its horn and the contours of the wrinkles around its snout.

On this particular day, Dr. Mbayma is observing an adult male rhino named M–5. The time is late afternoon, and M–5 is grazing after his midday sleep. Dr. Mbayma has found that white rhinos sleep mostly between 10 AM and 2 PM, when the temperature rises above 32°C. During the rest of the daylight hours, the rhinos eat—and eat!

M–5 may not know it, but he is lucky to be alive. Fifty years ago, Garamba National Park was set aside as a preserve for animals such as M–5, who is one of a rare subspecies of white rhinoceroses that are native to this part of Africa. At that time, more than 1000 of these animals were in existence. But by 1983, only 15 of M–5's relatives were left. What had happened? That question can be answered in one word: poaching.

Poaching is illegal hunting. When Garamba National Park was set aside as a wildlife preserve, guards were hired to make sure that the rhinos in the park would be free to live and reproduce. Many hunters, however, managed to outwit the guards and slaughtered the rhinos. To make matters worse, some corrupt guards joined the poachers, using their jobs as an easy way to get rich on bribes or as a source of free rhino meat.

The rewards for poaching run high. Today, a single horn from a white rhinoceros is valued at about $24,000. The value of the horn is based on the fact that it can be ground up for medicinal purposes or used to make decorative objects, just as elephant tusks are illegally sold for ivory. In addition to the valuable horn, rhinoceros meat is a tempting source of food for poor African villagers who have little nutritious food to eat.

With the white rhinoceros on the brink of extinction, conservation groups joined with the government of Zaire to clean up the corruption at Garamba. The first step was to hire a new park warden to replace the one who had been compromised by the poachers. The next step was to make the job of park guard attractive in terms of

▲ Poachers beware! Members of Dr. Mbayma Atalia's anti-poaching unit are setting off to patrol the 7800 square kilometers of Garamba National Park.

salary and other incentives. The final step was to engage highly motivated researchers, such as Dr. Mbayma, whose knowledge of the white rhino makes them ideally suited to serve as protection officers. An additional step has since been taken. The new park warden, Dr. Muhindo Mesi, has begun a program to help local villagers improve their sheep and goat herds so that they will not be tempted to poach rhinos for meat.

Today, Garamba National Park is a model for wildlife conservation in Africa. Not one white rhinoceros has been poached since 1984, and the birth of new animals has brought the total number of white rhinos at Garamba up to 26. In some African countries, the rhinos have totally disappeared. In others, their numbers have dropped alarmingly. Only in Zaire is the white rhinoceros population growing rather than shrinking. Thanks to people like Dr. Mbayma Atalia and Dr. Muhindo Mesi, Garamba National Park has succeeded where many other conservation efforts have failed.

SEA FLOOR MINERALS
WHO OWNS THEM?

Six hundred meters below the ocean's surface, the strange and beautiful world of underwater plants and animals is suddenly pierced by a powerful beam of light. The light illuminates a vast array of fish, other sea animals, and sea plants. These life forms represent just a few of the many treasures of the ocean depths.

The light, which is carried aboard a strange-looking diving suit called the Wasp, suddenly focuses on another buried treasure. Potato-sized lumps of rock cover the ocean bottom in many places. These rock lumps, or nodules, represent trillions of tons of minerals sitting on the ocean floor just waiting to be scooped up.

Geologists believe that more than 1.5 trillion tons of these nodules occur in the Pacific Ocean, with lesser amounts in the other oceans of the world. Scientists estimate that there may be more than $3 trillion worth of minerals in the nodules!

The nodules are rich in a variety of minerals, including manganese, copper, nickel, cobalt, tungsten, vanadium, tin, titanium, silver, platinum, and gold. Land reserves of these minerals are steadily being depleted. So harvesting the nodules from the ocean floor seems to be a sensible and perhaps even essential idea. Why then do the nodules remain unmined along the ocean floor as the need for the minerals continues to grow?

This vast and valuable natural resource remains untapped because two important questions remain unanswered: How can the minerals be mined, and who owns the right to mine the minerals? Scientists and world leaders are now trying to find answers to these questions.

Developing the technologies to recover the nodules needs careful research and testing. Several techniques to retrieve the nodules have already been tried, but the attempts have met with only partial success. One approach uses a series of huge metal buckets strung along a belt that moves between a ship and the ocean floor. The buckets

▼ **An ocean-mining ship, followed by an ore carrier, trails a dredge to scoop up mineral nodules from the ocean floor.**

▶ **Like a deep-sea conveyor belt, an underwater dredge scoops minerals from the ocean floor and transports them to the surface.**

▲ Superheated water, gases, and minerals pour out of a natural chimney, or "black smoker"—a deep-sea vent on the floor of the Pacific Ocean.

▲ Manganese nodules are part of the wealth of the ocean floor. Manganese is important in the manufacture of steel and other alloys.

scrape along the ocean floor, pick up the nodules, and carry them to the ship. Another method employs a giant vacuum that sucks up the ooze along the ocean bottom and the nodules as well. A third scheme involves the use of robots to find and retrieve the mineral treasures.

With technological advances, the problem of mining the minerals may soon be answered. But the international political questions still remain: Who has the right to mine the ocean depths? Where should this mining be allowed? Who should set the rules? And who should benefit from ocean mining?

These questions are difficult to answer. Since 1959, representatives from many nations have been meeting to try to create a Law of the Sea. This law would regulate ocean mining, oil drilling, fishing, energy usage, dumping of wastes, exploration, and research. Finally, in 1982, 119 nations signed a Law of the Sea treaty. But the United States was not one of them.

Under provisions of the treaty, each coastal nation is given an exclusive economic zone of 200 nautical miles from its shore.

Within that zone, a nation controls all natural resources, dumping, economic use, and scientific research. Where economic zones of different nations overlap, the nations must work out agreements.

Outside the economic zones, no single nation controls the ocean floor. The International Seabed Authority administers this vast ocean-floor region, called the International Seabed Area. The Authority sets the rules for mining in the International Seabed Area. And further, all mining technology must be shared with the Authority.

The United States could not accept these provisions and did not sign the Law of the Sea treaty. On March 10, 1983, the United States declared its own economic zone, extending 200 nautical miles off the coasts of the United States and all its territories.

Conflict over the zone has already arisen. And it is likely that many disputes will come up when people start mining the ocean floor for its mineral wealth. Who do you think should own these valuable and vital mineral resources?

PRISONERS UNDER PLASTIC

It was almost midnight by the time Lorraine finished her English report on twentieth-century British musicians of the 1960s.

"Enough homework," she mumbled to herself, "it's time to celebrate the New Year."

"Wake up, Grandpa," said Lorraine to the tall white-haired figure sleeping in an old but comfortable-looking lounge chair. "I'm turning on the video wall."

As she spoke, the glass wall that provided a view of the city from their seventieth-story apartment became a giant video screen.

> ▼ Is this a frightening preview of Earth in the twenty-third century? The choices we make today will affect the way our grandchildren live in the future.

In the distance, both Lorraine and her grandfather could hear the computerized electronic version of "Auld Lang Syne" bounce off the roof of the city and reflect from skyscraper to skyscraper, changing pitch from street to street.

"Just think, Grandpa, it's finally here—the twenty-third century!"

Before her grandfather could respond, the video screen switched to a news bulletin. Lorraine and her grandfather watched intently as the newscaster told of another daring attempt by a group called the Outsiders to break out of the city complex.

"Why do they keep trying to escape the city?" murmured Lorraine, without really expecting an answer. "After all, the air and water are poisonous out there, and the land is totally barren. No one can survive outside the protective dome of our city. Don't they know that?"

Lorraine's grandfather smiled, but it was a sad, knowing smile.

"They know," he whispered. "I can remember a time when everyone lived outside—a time before we became prisoners under a plastic dome. Back then you could swim in the rivers, breathe the fresh mountain air, and admire the plants and wildlife that flourished in the forests."

"I don't see why you call us prisoners," answered Lorraine glibly. "What could be better than the year-round perfect environment in our city? Besides, I don't believe you've ever been outside—no one's ever been outside. It's the law."

Lorraine's grandfather started to argue. He wanted to tell her about the joys of walking through the sand along the seashore on a sunny day or watching snow falling on a winter's night. And he wanted to teach her about the pollution that had ruined Earth's rivers and atmosphere and killed off just about all living things outside the domed environments—pollution and destruction that occurred long before she was born. But he stopped himself in time.

"No point in telling her what she's missing," he whispered to himself, "she'll never be able to experience it anyway." A single tear slid down his cheek. "How sad never to feel the wind on your face."

"Cheer up, Grandpa. A new century is about to begin. Isn't life wonderful?"

For Further Reading

If you have been intrigued by the concepts examined in this textbook, you may also be interested in the ways fellow thinkers—novelists, poets, essayists, as well as scientists—have imaginatively explored the same ideas.

Chapter 1: Energy Resources

Beatty, Patricia. *Jonathan Down Under*. New York: Morrow.

Engdahl, Sylvia. *This Star Shall Abide*. New York: Atheneum.

Perez, Norah H. *Breaker*. Boston, MA: Houghton Mifflin.

Sharpe, Susan. *Waterman's Boy*. New York: Bradbury.

Chapter 2: Earth's Nonliving Resources

Collier, James Lincoln. *When the Stars Begin to Fall*. New York: Delacorte Press.

Hamilton, Virginia. *M.C. Higgins, the Great*. New York: Macmillan.

Rubinstein, Robert E. *When Sirens Scream*. New York: Dodd, Mead.

Sargent, Sarah. *Seeds of Change*. New York: Bradbury.

White, Robb. *Deathwatch*. Garden City, NY: Doubleday.

Chapter 3: Pollution

Chester, Aaron. *Spill*. New York: Atheneum.

George, Jean. *Who Really Killed Cock Robin?* New York: Dutton.

Moeri, Louise. *Downwind*. New York: Dutton.

Swindells, Robert. *A Serpent's Tooth*. New York: Holiday House.

Thiele, Colin. *Fight Against Albatross Two*. New York: Harper & Row.

Chapter 4: Conserving Earth's Resources

Bond, Nancy. *The Voyage Begun*. New York: Atheneum.

St. George, Judith. *Do You See What I See?* New York: Putnam.

Sampson, Fay. *The Watch on Patterick Fell*. New York: Greenwillow.

Shute, Nevil. *On the Beach*. New York: Morrow.

Strieber, Whitley. *Wolf of Shadows*. New York: Knopf.

Appendix A

The metric system of measurement is used by scientists throughout the world. It is based on units of ten. Each unit is ten times larger or ten times smaller than the next unit. The most commonly used units of the metric system are given below. After you have finished reading about the metric system, try to put it to use. How tall are you in metrics? What is your mass? What is your normal body temperature in degrees Celsius?

Commonly Used Metric Units

Length The distance from one point to another

meter (m)   A meter is slightly longer than a yard.
              1 meter = 1000 millimeters (mm)
              1 meter = 100 centimeters (cm)
              1000 meters = 1 kilometer (km)

Volume The amount of space an object takes up

liter (L)   A liter is slightly more than a quart.
              1 liter = 1000 milliliters (mL)

Mass The amount of matter in an object

gram (g)   A gram has a mass equal to about one paper clip.
              1000 grams = 1 kilogram (kg)

Temperature The measure of hotness or coldness

degrees   0°C = freezing point of water
Celsius (°C)   100°C = boiling point of water

Metric–English Equivalents

2.54 centimeters (cm) = 1 inch (in.)
1 meter (m) = 39.37 inches (in.)
1 kilometer (km) = 0.62 miles (mi)
1 liter (L) = 1.06 quarts (qt)
250 milliliters (mL) = 1 cup (c)
1 kilogram (kg) = 2.2 pounds (lb)
28.3 grams (g) = 1 ounce (oz)
$°C = 5/9 \times (°F - 32)$

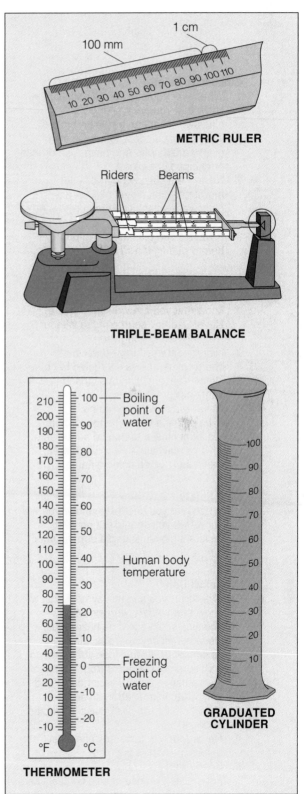

METRIC RULER

TRIPLE-BEAM BALANCE

THERMOMETER

GRADUATED CYLINDER

Glassware Safety
1. Whenever you see this symbol, you will know that you are working with glassware that can easily be broken. Take particular care to handle such glassware safely. And never use broken or chipped glassware.
2. Never heat glassware that is not thoroughly dry. Never pick up any glassware unless you are sure it is not hot. If it is hot, use heat-resistant gloves.
3. Always clean glassware thoroughly before putting it away.

Fire Safety
1. Whenever you see this symbol, you will know that you are working with fire. Never use any source of fire without wearing safety goggles.
2. Never heat anything—particularly chemicals—unless instructed to do so.
3. Never heat anything in a closed container.
4. Never reach across a flame.
5. Always use a clamp, tongs, or heat-resistant gloves to handle hot objects.
6. Always maintain a clean work area, particularly when using a flame.

Heat Safety
Whenever you see this symbol, you will know that you should put on heat-resistant gloves to avoid burning your hands.

Chemical Safety
1. Whenever you see this symbol, you will know that you are working with chemicals that could be hazardous.
2. Never smell any chemical directly from its container. Always use your hand to waft some of the odors from the top of the container toward your nose—and only when instructed to do so.
3. Never mix chemicals unless instructed to do so.
4. Never touch or taste any chemical unless instructed to do so.
5. Keep all lids closed when chemicals are not in use. Dispose of all chemicals as instructed by your teacher.

6. Immediately rinse with water any chemicals, particularly acids, that get on your skin and clothes. Then notify your teacher.

Eye and Face Safety
1. Whenever you see this symbol, you will know that you are performing an experiment in which you must take precautions to protect your eyes and face by wearing safety goggles.
2. When you are heating a test tube or bottle, always point it away from you and others. Chemicals can splash or boil out of a heated test tube.

Sharp Instrument Safety
1. Whenever you see this symbol, you will know that you are working with a sharp instrument.
2. Always use single-edged razors; double-edged razors are too dangerous.
3. Handle any sharp instrument with extreme care. Never cut any material toward you; always cut away from you.
4. Immediately notify your teacher if your skin is cut.

Electrical Safety
1. Whenever you see this symbol, you will know that you are using electricity in the laboratory.
2. Never use long extension cords to plug in any electrical device. Do not plug too many appliances into one socket or you may overload the socket and cause a fire.
3. Never touch an electrical appliance or outlet with wet hands.

Animal Safety
1. Whenever you see this symbol, you will know that you are working with live animals.
2. Do not cause pain, discomfort, or injury to an animal.
3. Follow your teacher's directions when handling animals. Wash your hands thoroughly after handling animals or their cages.

One of the first things a scientist learns is that working in the laboratory can be an exciting experience. But the laboratory can also be quite dangerous if proper safety rules are not followed at all times. To prepare yourself for a safe year in the laboratory, read over the following safety rules. Then read them a second time. Make sure you understand each rule. If you do not, ask your teacher to explain any rules you are unsure of.

Dress Code

1. Many materials in the laboratory can cause eye injury. To protect yourself from possible injury, wear safety goggles whenever you are working with chemicals, burners, or any substance that might get into your eyes. Never wear contact lenses in the laboratory.

2. Wear a laboratory apron or coat whenever you are working with chemicals or heated substances.

3. Tie back long hair to keep it away from any chemicals, burners and candles, or other laboratory equipment.

4. Remove or tie back any article of clothing or jewelry that can hang down and touch chemicals and flames.

General Safety Rules

5. Read all directions for an experiment several times. Follow the directions exactly as they are written. If you are in doubt about any part of the experiment, ask your teacher for assistance.

6. Never perform activities that are not authorized by your teacher. Obtain permission before "experimenting" on your own.

7. Never handle any equipment unless you have specific permission.

8. Take extreme care not to spill any material in the laboratory. If a spill occurs, immediately ask your teacher about the proper cleanup procedure. Never simply pour chemicals or other substances into the sink or trash container.

9. Never eat in the laboratory.

10. Wash your hands before and after each experiment.

First Aid

11. Immediately report all accidents, no matter how minor, to your teacher.

12. Learn what to do in case of specific accidents, such as getting acid in your eyes or on your skin. (Rinse acids from your body with lots of water.)

13. Become aware of the location of the first-aid kit. But your teacher should administer any required first aid due to injury. Or your teacher may send you to the school nurse or call a physician.

14. Know where and how to report an accident or fire. Find out the location of the fire extinguisher, phone, and fire alarm. Keep a list of important phone numbers—such as the fire department and the school nurse—near the phone. Immediately report any fires to your teacher.

Heating and Fire Safety

15. Again, never use a heat source, such as a candle or burner, without wearing safety goggles.

16. Never heat a chemical you are not instructed to heat. A chemical that is harmless when cool may be dangerous when heated.

17. Maintain a clean work area and keep all materials away from flames.

18. Never reach across a flame.

19. Make sure you know how to light a Bunsen burner. (Your teacher will demonstrate the proper procedure for lighting a burner.) If the flame leaps out of a burner toward you, immediately turn off the gas. Do not touch the burner. It may be hot. And never leave a lighted burner unattended!

20. When heating a test tube or bottle, always point it away from you and others. Chemicals can splash or boil out of a heated test tube.

21. Never heat a liquid in a closed container. The expanding gases produced may blow the container apart, injuring you or others.

22. Before picking up a container that has been heated, first hold the back of your hand near it. If you can feel the heat on the back of your hand, the container may be too hot to handle. Use a clamp or tongs when handling hot containers.

Using Chemicals Safely

23. Never mix chemicals for the "fun of it." You might produce a dangerous, possibly explosive substance.

24. Never touch, taste, or smell a chemical unless you are instructed by your teacher to do so. Many chemicals are poisonous. If you are instructed to note the fumes in an experiment, gently wave your hand over the opening of a container and direct the fumes toward your nose. Do not inhale the fumes directly from the container.

25. Use only those chemicals needed in the activity. Keep all lids closed when a chemical is not being used. Notify your teacher whenever chemicals are spilled.

26. Dispose of all chemicals as instructed by your teacher. To avoid contamination, never return chemicals to their original containers.

27. Be extra careful when working with acids or bases. Pour such chemicals over the sink, not over your workbench.

28. When diluting an acid, pour the acid into water. Never pour water into an acid.

29. Immediately rinse with water any acids that get on your skin or clothing. Then notify your teacher of any acid spill.

Using Glassware Safely

30. Never force glass tubing into a rubber stopper. A turning motion and lubricant will be helpful when inserting glass tubing into rubber stoppers or rubber tubing. Your teacher will demonstrate the proper way to insert glass tubing.

31. Never heat glassware that is not thoroughly dry. Use a wire screen to protect glassware from any flame.

32. Keep in mind that hot glassware will not appear hot. Never pick up glassware without first checking to see if it is hot. See #22.

33. If you are instructed to cut glass tubing, fire-polish the ends immediately to remove sharp edges.

34. Never use broken or chipped glassware. If glassware breaks, notify your teacher and dispose of the glassware in the proper trash container.

35. Never eat or drink from laboratory glassware. Thoroughly clean glassware before putting it away.

Using Sharp Instruments

36. Handle scalpels or razor blades with extreme care. Never cut material toward you; cut away from you.

37. Immediately notify your teacher if you cut your skin when working in the laboratory.

Animal Safety

38. No experiments that will cause pain, discomfort, or harm to mammals, birds, reptiles, fishes, and amphibians should be done in the classroom or at home.

39. Animals should be handled only if necessary. If an animal is excited or frightened, pregnant, feeding, or with its young, special handling is required.

40. Your teacher will instruct you as to how to handle each animal species that may be brought into the classroom.

41. Clean your hands thoroughly after handling animals or the cage containing animals.

End-of-Experiment Rules

42. After an experiment has been completed, clean up your work area and return all equipment to its proper place.

43. Wash your hands after every experiment.

44. Turn off all burners before leaving the laboratory. Check that the gas line leading to the burner is off as well.

Glossary

Pronunciation Key

When difficult names or terms first appear in the text, they are respelled to aid pronunciation. A syllable in SMALL CAPITAL LETTERS receives the most stress. The key below lists the letters used for respelling. It includes examples of words using each sound and shows how the words would be respelled.

Symbol	Example	Respelling
a	hat	(hat)
ay	pay, late	(pay), (layt)
ah	star, hot	(stahr), (haht)
ai	air, dare	(air), (dair)
aw	law, all	(law), (awl)
eh	met	(meht)
ee	bee, eat	(bee), (eet)
er	learn, sir, fur	(lern), (ser), (fer)
ih	fit	(fiht)
igh	mile, sigh	(mighl), (sigh)
oh	no	(noh)
oi	soil, boy	(soil), (boi)
oo	root, rule	(root), (rool)
or	born, door	(born), (dor)
ow	plow, out	(plow), (owt)

Symbol	Example	Respelling
u	put, book	(put), (buk)
uh	fun	(fuhn)
yoo	few, use	(fyoo), (yooz)
ch	chill, reach	(chihl), (reech)
g	go, dig	(goh), (dihg)
j	jet, gently, bridge	(jeht), (JEHNTlee), (brihj)
k	kite, cup	(kight), (kuhp)
ks	mix	(mihks)
kw	quick	(kwihk)
ng	bring	(brihng)
s	say, cent	(say), (sehnt)
sh	she, crash	(shee), (krash)
th	three	(three)
y	yet, onion	(yeht), (UHN yuhn)
z	zip, always	(zihp), (AWL wayz)
zh	treasure	(TREH zher)

acid rain: general term used for precipitation (rain, snow, sleet, hail, or fog) that is more acidic than normal

alloy: substance made of two or more metals

anthracite (AN-thruh-sight): hard coal; fourth and last stage in the development of coal

biomass: any material, such as wood, that comes from living things and can be used as a fuel

bituminous (bigh-TOO-muh-nuhs) **coal:** soft coal; third stage in the development of coal

catalytic converter: emission-control device that changes hydrocarbons and carbon monoxide in automobile exhaust into carbon dioxide and water vapor

chain reaction: process in which the splitting, or fission, of one atomic nucleus causes the splitting of additional nuclei

combustion: process in which hydrocarbons in fossil fuels are combined with oxygen at high temperatures, releasing heat energy and light energy; burning

conservation: wise use of natural resources so they will not be used up too quickly or used in a way that will damage the environment

contour plowing: planting crops along the face, or side, of a slope instead of up and down the slope to prevent erosion

crop rotation: process of alternating crops on the same land to prevent depletion of nutrients from the soil

depletion: removal of nutrients from the soil

desalination (dee-sal-uh-NAY-shuhn): process by which salt is removed from ocean water

desertification (dih-zert-uh-fih-KAY-shuhn): process by which grasslands become deserts as a result of erosion caused by overgrazing

emissions (ee-MIHSH-uhnz): gases or particles given off when fossil fuels are burned

erosion: carrying off of soil by water or wind

fossil fuel: fuel formed hundreds of millions of years ago from the remains of dead plants and animals; coal, oil, or natural gas

gasohol: mixture of gasoline and alcohol that can be used as a fuel

geothermal energy: energy produced from the heat energy within the Earth

groundwater: water in the soil

hazardous waste: any waste that can cause death or serious damage to human health; toxic, or poisonous, chemical waste

hydrocarbon: substance containing the elements hydrogen and carbon

hydroelectric power: use of mechanical energy of falling or running water to generate electricity

irrigation (eer-uh-GAY-shuhn): process of supplying water to dry regions to make them suitable for growing crops

lignite (LIHG-night): brown coal; second stage in the development of coal

mineral: naturally occurring chemical substance found in soil or rocks

natural resource: any material removed from the Earth and used by people

nonpoint source: source of water pollution that may include sanitary landfills, hazardous wastes, and agricultural runoff

nonrenewable resource: any resource that cannot be replaced by nature, such as fossil fuels and minerals

nuclear energy: energy locked within the atomic nucleus

nuclear fission: splitting of an atomic nucleus into two smaller nuclei, during which nuclear energy is released

nuclear fusion: combining two atomic nuclei to produce one larger nucleus, with the release of nuclear energy

nucleus: center, or core, of an atom; plural, nuclei

ore: deposit of a mineral that can be mined at a profit

peat: soft substance made of decayed plant fibers; first stage in the development of coal

petrochemical: any useful substance derived from oil or natural gas

photovoltaic cell: device that converts sunlight directly into electricity; solar cell

point source: source of water pollution that may include sewers, pipes, and channels through which wastes are discharged

pollution: release into the environment of substances that change the environment for the worse

radioactive waste: waste produced by the production of energy in nuclear power plants

recycling: form of conservation in which discarded materials that can be used again are separated and sent to factories where they are reclaimed

renewable resource: any resource that can be replaced by nature, such as water, soil, and living resources

sanitary landfill: solid-waste dump in which garbage is compacted and covered with soil

smog: thick brownish haze formed when hydrocarbons, carbon monoxide, and other gases react in sunlight; combination of the words smoke and fog

solar collector: device that absorbs energy from the sun and converts it to heat; part of an active solar-heating system

solar energy: energy from the sun

strip cropping: planting strips of cover crops, such as clover, between rows of other crops, such as corn, to prevent erosion

temperature inversion: phenomenon that occurs when cool air containing pollutants becomes trapped near the Earth's surface under a layer of warm air

terracing: planting a slope in a series of level steps, or terraces, to prevent erosion

thermal pollution: increase in temperature caused when cold water used to cool the reactors in nuclear power plants is heated and discharged back into lakes and rivers

tidal energy: energy produced by the rise and fall of the tides

water cycle: movement of water from the Earth's surface to the atmosphere and back to the surface

Index

Credits

SVP
RAINTREE
STECK-VAUGHN
PUBLISHERS
A Steck-Vaughn Company
Austin, Texas
www.steck-vaughn.com

A LOOK AT LIFE IN

The Sixties

R. G. Grant

Published by Raintree Steck-Vaughn Publishers,
an imprint of Steck-Vaughn Company

Printed in Italy. Bound in the United States.
1 2 3 4 5 6 7 8 9 0 04 03 02 01 00

Library of Congress Cataloging-in-Publication Data
Grant, R. G.
The Sixties / R. G. Grant.
    p.   cm.—(A look at life in)
    Includes bibliographical references and index.
    ISBN 0-7398-1339-0
    1. Civilization, Modern, --1950—Juvenile literature.
    2. Nineteen sixties—Juvenile literature.
    3. Popular culture—History—20th century—
Juvenile literature.
    I. Title. II. Series.
    CB429.G735 2000
    909.82'6—dc21   99-36359

Cover photographs

Top left: West Berliners wave across the
Berlin Wall, 1961. (Popperfoto)

Top right: The Beatles, 1963
(Popperfoto)

Center: Leonard Nimoy as Mr. Spock
in *Star Trek* (Kobal Collection)

Bottom left: Hippies at a "happening,"
selling beads, bells, and badges.
(Topham Picturepoint)

Bottom right: Astronaut "Buzz" Aldrin
on the Moon, July 1969, with the
reflection of Neil Armstrong in his
helmet (Popperfoto)

Acknowledgments

The Author and Publishers thank the following for
their permission to reproduce photographs: Camera
Press: pages 10, 12t, 16b, 18b, 19, 22tr, 22b, 29b,
41b; Hulton Getty: pages 5, 6b, 7b, 9, 11b, 12b, 17,
18t, 23, 30t; Kobal Collection: pages 38t, 38b, 39t,
39b; Popperfoto: pages 4b, 6t, 7t, 8t, 8b, 11t, 13b,
14b, 21t, 22tl, 25, 26t, 32t, 32b, 33, 34t, 35t, 35b,
37t; Retna Pictures: pages 24t, 24b, 26b, 27b, 37b;
Topham Picturepoint: pages 4t, 14t, 15t, 16t, 20l,
21bl, 27t, 28b, 29t, 30b, 36, 40, 41t; Corbis-
Bettmann: pages 13t, 20t, 21b, 31.

Contents

A Look at...

...in the '60s

A LOOK AT
THE NEWS
IN THE '60s

A famous song of the 1960s, by Bob Dylan, was "The Times They Are A-Changin'." There was a feeling of optimism, a sense that life could be changed for the better. In North America and Western Europe, at least, people were better off than ever before. Jobs were plentiful, and every year there were more consumer goods that ordinary families could afford to buy. But the decade was also a time of bitter social conflicts and brutal warfare.

Young people and the "generation gap"

Society was full of young people. A high birth rate in the late 1940s and early 1950s meant that schools and universities were expanding. With more money in their pockets, young people had more independence. Many rejected the hard-working, conservative way in which their parents had lived. They wanted more fun. The "generation gap" between teenagers and their parents was endlessly debated.

Hippies

In the mid-1960s the Hippie movement grew up in the Haight Ashbury section of San Francisco.

Profile

Che Guevara

Many students in the later 1960s had a poster of Argentinian-born revolutionary Ernesto "Che" Guevara on their walls. He was the right-hand man of Fidel Castro, who had carried out a successful revolution in Cuba in 1959. In 1965 Guevara left Cuba to spark revolutions around the world. He tried to start an uprising in Bolivia and was killed there in 1967.

Che's example appealed to young people who had a romantic view of the need for a revolution to change the world for the better.

...Newsflash...

Monterey, June 1967. Since the start of this year, the children of white middle-class families have been tuning in to Flower Power. At mass open-air festivals, beginning with a "Be-In" in San Francisco, thousands have been introduced to the chanting of mantras and smoking marijuana. Now they are calling this the "Summer of Love," as young people with flowers in their hair flock to music events like the International Pop Festival at Monterey.

Hippies wanted to create an ideal world based on peace and love, in which there would be no money and no work. Few people tried to live a full Hippie lifestyle, but many were influenced by their "flower power" attitudes.

Young people and politics

Some young people, especially students, became involved in political protest. Many students felt that the older generation had ruined the world with wars, racism, pollution, and a joyless lifestyle. Some decided that the answer was a revolution in the way society was run. In 1968, France was brought to a standstill by student uprisings, and there were major disruptions also in Germany, Italy, and the United States.

Tennessee Williams said of this period:

"The sixties were a decade of great vitality....The civil rights movement, the movement against war and imperialism....Then we had brave people fighting against privilege and injustice."

▷ *Riot police charge student demonstrators in Paris, June 1968. Many protesters were injured and killed in confrontations with police.*

△ *Soviet tanks in Prague, Czechoslovakia, in August 1968*

In Northern Ireland, students took the lead in protests in favor of equal rights for Catholics. The movement met with a violent reaction from Protestants, which led to British troops being sent to the streets in 1969.

Young people were in the forefront of the "Prague Spring" of 1968, when communist Czechoslovakia was swept by a movement for liberal reform. However, the reform movement was soon crushed. Troops from the Soviet Union and its allies invaded Czechoslovakia and restored the old communist order.

In communist China, in 1966, dictator Mao Tse-tung encouraged young people, the Red Guards, to attack teachers and other authority figures in what was called the Cultural Revolution.

The Cold War

The Cold War was a period of tension between the United States and the Soviet Union. Both sides had nuclear weapons ready for delivery against each other's cities at a minute's notice. In the early 1960s both sides carried out nuclear tests, exploding devices that scattered nuclear fallout into the atmosphere.

The United States and the Soviet Union ran large espionage organizations, the CIA and the KGB, which often made headlines. In 1960 a U.S. U2 spy plane was shot down over the Soviet Union, and its pilot, Gary Powers, was captured. In 1963, a spy scandal rocked British politics when it turned out that the defense minister, John Profumo, had been sharing a girlfriend with a Soviet spy.

▷ *Red Guards in Peking carry images of Mao Tse-tung, August 1966.*

The Iron Curtain and the Berlin Wall

An "Iron Curtain" was said to divide the communist countries of Eastern Europe from democratic Western Europe. The Iron Curtain went through the German city of Berlin, which was jointly controlled by NATO countries (Great Britain, France, and the United States) and the Soviet Union.

In 1961 the Soviets and their East German allies built a wall across the center of Berlin, dividing the Soviet-controlled zone of the city from the NATO-controlled zone. Many people died trying to cross the Berlin Wall, to escape from the Communist East into West Berlin.

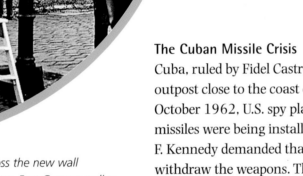

△ West Berliners wave across the new wall that divided Berlin. A little later, East German police would throw tear gas grenades over the wall, to prevent even this contact between West and East.

The Cuban Missile Crisis

Cuba, ruled by Fidel Castro, was a communist outpost close to the coast of the United States. In October 1962, U.S. spy planes discovered that Soviet missiles were being installed in Cuba. President John F. Kennedy demanded that the Soviet Union withdraw the weapons. The world came close to nuclear war. But, after tense negotiations, the Soviet Union gave in.

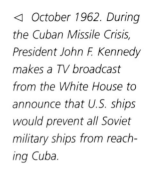

◁ October 1962. During the Cuban Missile Crisis, President John F. Kennedy makes a TV broadcast from the White House to announce that U.S. ships would prevent all Soviet military ships from reaching Cuba.

The U.S. war in Vietnam

The 1960s was a troubled decade for the United States. The country became involved in a major war in Vietnam, which was divided into a communist-ruled state of North Vietnam and a pro-American South Vietnam. Hundreds of thousands of U.S. troops, plus air and naval power, were used in an attempt to stop a communist takeover in South Vietnam. By 1970, almost 50,000 Americans had died in Vietnam, without achieving victory. The war caused bitter controversy in the United States. Many young people joined antiwar demonstrations.

John Levin, a student leader in San Francisco, said:

"We'd been brought up to believe ... that America fought on the side of justice .... So, along with the absolute horror of the war in Vietnam, there was also a feeling of personal betrayal. I remember crying ... late at night in my room, listening to the reports of the war."

△ *A U.S. soldier in Hue, South Vietnam, comforts a wounded comrade, 1968.*

Assassinations

The single most dramatic event of the decade was the assassination of President John F. Kennedy in 1963. An official inquiry held that he was killed by a lone sniper, Lee Harvey Oswald—who was himself shot dead, two days after Kennedy's death, while in police custody.

President Kennedy's brother, Robert Kennedy, was also assassinated, in 1968. So was the African-American Civil Rights leader, Martin Luther King, Jr.

▽ *November 22, 1963. The assassination of President Kennedy as he rode through Dallas in a convertible was caught on film by an amateur photographer. Kennedy's wife, Jackie (in pink), holds her husband.*

...Newsflash...

Washington, DC, August 28, 1963. Martin Luther King, Jr. today addressed the largest Civil Rights protest ever, as 200,000 demonstrators responded to his call for a March on Washington. Celebrities, including Marlon Brando, Bob Dylan, and Judy Garland, were there to support the call for equal rights for America's black population. At the Lincoln Memorial, King told the crowd: "I have a dream that all God's children, black men and white men, Jews and Gentiles, Protestants and Catholics, will be able to join hands ..."

Civil Rights and Black Power

The Civil Rights movement in the United States, led by Martin Luther King, Jr., was a campaign for equal rights for African Americans. Many whites in the southern states violently resisted desegregation—allowing blacks to use the same schools and other public facilities as whites. They also resisted giving blacks the right to vote. By the end of the decade, new laws and direct action by African Americans had largely given blacks the rights they deserved. But this did not end racial tension.

At first, most African Americans followed King in his nonviolence and his desire for a "color-blind" society. Later in the 1960s, the more aggressive Black Power movement emerged. It asserted the distinct qualities of black people. There was a series of large-scale riots in black ghettos in U.S. cities between 1964 and 1968.

▽ *Martin Luther King, Jr. and his wife lead a Civil Rights march in Alabama, 1965. Inspired by the ideas of Indian campaigner Mahatma Gandhi, King stuck to nonviolent methods of protest, even when his enemies resorted to extreme violence.*

South Africa and Rhodesia

At the start of the 1960s, many countries in Africa and the West Indies were still ruled by Europeans. Most of these colonies became independent during the decade. But in southern Africa, a white minority continued to rule the black majority.

In South Africa, the apartheid system gave whites complete political and economic power over the black majority. Opposition to apartheid was led by the African National Congress (ANC). In 1964 its leader, Nelson Mandela, was sentenced to life imprisonment by a South African court.

In the British colony of Rhodesia (now Zimbabwe), whites declared independence under a white-only government, to prevent Great Britain from holding elections that would have brought in a black government.

Good-bye
De Gaulle, president of France (resigned 1969)

Hello
Mrs. Sirimavo Bandaranaike, prime minister of Ceylon, 1960; Jomo Kenyatta, president of Kenya, 1964; Leonid Brezhnev, leader of USSR, 1964

Racism in Europe

Racism was also a problem in Europe. Millions of immigrants from the former colonies started new lives in European countries. They were often not welcomed. In Great Britain, the government passed laws to limit immigration and also tried to ban racial prejudice.

▽ *There were separate stairways for whites and nonwhites at the railroad station in Johannesburg, South Africa.*

...Newsflash...

Pretoria, June 14, 1964. Nelson Mandela, one of the leaders of the struggle against South Africa's racist apartheid regime, was today sentenced to life imprisonment. He has been sent to Robben Island, a prison from which no escape is possible. But Mandela has refused to give up hope. In a powerful speech to the court, he said he still believed in a democratic and free society. "It is an ideal I hope to live for and achieve," he said. "But if needs be, it is an ideal for which I am prepared to die."

NIE BLANKES
NON-WHITES

Profile

Indira Gandhi

Indira Gandhi was the daughter of India's first prime minister, Jawaharlal Nehru, She played an important role in the struggle for Indian independence from British rule in the 1940s. By the start of the 1960s, she was president of Congress, India's main political party. In January 1966, she became prime minister.

To have a woman as leader of the government in one of the world's largest countries was a great step forward for women everywhere. Indira Gandhi dominated Indian politics for almost 20 years. She was assassinated in 1984.

Women's rights

Women began to challenge their position in society. In 1963 feminist Betty Friedan wrote *The Feminine Mystique*, attacking the idea that women should be happy simply being housewives and mothers. She also founded the National Organization for Women (NOW), which campaigned for women's rights in the United States.

A few powerful women leaders emerged, notably Indira Gandhi, prime minister of India from 1966, and Golda Meir, who became Israeli prime minister in 1969.

Liberalization

The 1960s was a decade of liberalization. For example, capital punishment was abolished in many European and South American countries. Censorship was relaxed. Abortion and homosexuality were legalized. People had different views about whether these measures were signs of progress. But times certainly were changing.

▽ *Betty Friedan, a leader of the women's liberation movement in the United States, addresses a meeting in New York City.*

A LOOK AT
SCIENCE and TECHNOLOGY
IN THE '60s

Space exploration was the most impressive development in technology in the 1960s. At the start of the decade, no human being had ever left Earth's atmosphere. By the decade's end, humans had walked on the moon.

Competition between the United States and the Soviet Union was the driving force behind the Space Race. On April 12, 1961, the Soviet Union put cosmonaut Yuri Gagarin into orbit around the earth aboard spacecraft *Vostok 1*. In response, President John F. Kennedy promised that the United States would land a man on the moon before the decade was out.

▽ *Soviet leader Nikita Khrushchev (second from right) enjoys the cheers of a crowd for a line of Soviet cosmonauts: (from left) Popovich, Titov, Nikolaev, Gagarin, Tereshkova (the first woman in space, June 1963), and Bykovsky.*

Few people believed it could be done. But the U.S. government invested massive resources in its Apollo space program. There turned out to be no fundamental obstacles to space travel. On July 20, 1969, U.S. astronaut Neil Armstrong stepped onto the moon's surface.

Profile

John Glenn

▽ *John Glenn (left) with Vice-President Lyndon Johnson, 1962*

Astronaut John Glenn was already 38 years old when he joined the U.S. space program in 1959. He had fought as a Marine in World War II and had flown supersonic aircraft. On February 20, 1962, he became the first American to orbit the earth. On board the *Friendship 7* spacecraft, he completed three orbits before landing in the Atlantic Ocean. Glenn later entered politics, becoming a senator in 1975. In 1998, at the age of 77, he returned to space on board a shuttle.

◁ *Crowds in New York City's Grand Central Station watch as John Glenn goes into orbit around the earth in 1962.*

▽ *Apollo 11 astronaut Edwin "Buzz" Aldrin unpacks equipment on the moon, 1969.*

Firsts in the Space Race

For a while the Soviet Union stayed ahead in the Space Race. Soviet cosmonaut Alexei Leonov made the first space walk in March 1965, before Edward White became the first American to walk in space in June. The Soviet spacecraft *Luna 9* softlanded on the moon in February 1966, four months ahead of the U.S. *Surveyor 1*. But the Soviet Union never attempted a program of manned flights to the moon. In 1968 three U.S. astronauts made the first manned moon orbit, and in July 1969, astronauts Aldrin and Armstrong set the American flag on the moon.

...Newsflash...

July 20, 1969. Hundreds of millions of people around the world watched on television tonight as U.S. astronaut Neil Armstrong stepped out of lunar module Eagle and onto the surface of the moon. Armstrong told the watching millions: "That's one small step for a man, one giant leap for mankind." Another member of the *Apollo 11* team, Edwin "Buzz" Aldrin, later joined Armstrong on his historic moon walk.

◁ *The Early Bird satellite during a test before its launch in 1965*

Marshall McLuhan, one of the most admired thinkers of the 1960s, said that television and other electronic communications were recreating the world

"...in the image of a global village."

Computers

Computers were another area that made enormous progress through the space program, since they were needed to control space vehicles. However, computers were still large and astonishingly expensive machines, for use only by governments and business corporations. Personal computers and computer games did not begin to arrive until the 1970s.

▽ *Loading tapes for storing data onto a one-ton computer, 1966*

Communications

The space program had a huge impact on communications. But, in the early 1960s, communications were very poor by today's standards. For example, when President Kennedy was assassinated in 1963, no television pictures from the scene were available in Great Britain until the following day.

Communications were transformed by satellites. One, called Telstar, put into orbit in 1962, allowed the first live TV broadcasts across the Atlantic. But Telstar could transmit images for only a few minutes at a time.

The real turning point was the launch of the Early Bird satellite in 1965. It could be used for communications 24 hours a day. Once a series of similar satellites was in orbit at different locations, instant global communications became a reality.

△ *New models on display at the International Motor Show, 1961*

Technology at home

Technology at home was limited. Most people outside the United States still did not have a telephone at home. In 1964, only about one in 20 U.S. households had color televisions—which at first were expensive and not readily available. In Great Britain only the new channel, BBC2, broadcast in color in the 1960s.

Transportation

Jet air travel, begun in the 1950s, was developing rapidly. In tune with the space age, Great Britain and France cooperated to build a supersonic airliner, Concorde. The fastest passenger aircraft ever, it made its first test flight in 1969. But in the same year Boeing introduced the "jumbo jet," the Boeing 747. By

Good-bye
Steam trains
Ocean liners

Hello
Mont Blanc tunnel;
The *QE2* (ship);
Supertankers;
Concorde, and 747s

carrying more passengers in a single aircraft, the 747 helped make air travel affordable. This turned out to be as important as traveling faster.

The number of cars increased sharply, and many new roads were built. Cities were transformed by networks of highways and overpasses. But smaller cars became fashionable, and people became more safety conscious. This was partly due to activist Ralph Nader's book, *Unsafe at Any Speed*, 1965. It attacked the safety record of U.S. automobile manufacturers. Car seat belts were invented in the 1960s but were not widely used.

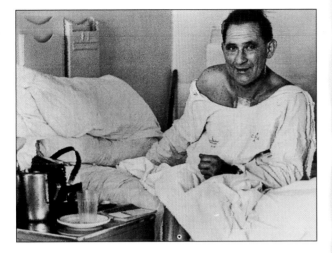

△ *Louis Washkansky survived for 18 days after his heart transplant operation.*

Cape Town, December 3, 1967. A South African surgeon, Christiaan Barnard, has carried out the world's first successful heart transplant operation. The patient, a 53-year-old grocer, Louis Washkansky, has been given the heart of a 25-year-old woman who died in a car accident. It is doubtful that Washkansky will live long, but once this new form of surgery is fully developed, it could save thousands of lives.

Life studies

A revolution in the study of life and the body was beginning with a new understanding of genetics. In 1962, U.S. scientist James Watson and British scientist Francis Crick were awarded the Nobel Prize for their work on DNA. They unraveled the genetic code that carries the information to build new organisms, including human beings.

It was a time of major medical progress. In particular, there were advances in dealing with heart disease. Surgeons carried out the first heart bypass operations and inserted the first electronic pacemakers. In 1967, a South African surgeon, Christiaan Barnard, was responsible for the first successful heart transplant operation.

▷ *People in the Democratic Republic of the Congo (Zaire) are vaccinated against smallpox.*

Preventing diseases

There was also progress in the prevention of disease. Campaigns against cigarette smoking got under way, after scientists officially confirmed that there was a link between smoking and cancer.

In many parts of the developing world, vaccination campaigns began to eradicate killer diseases such as smallpox.

Population growth

One result of medical progress was population growth. The steepest rise in world population in human history was taking place, concentrated mostly in the developing countries. Much effort was devoted to ideas for limiting population growth. This was the background to the birth control pill, developed by American Gregory Pincus in the 1950s and authorized for general use during the 1960s.

The environment

Population growth was one factor behind mounting concern about the human impact on the environment. In her book *Silent Spring*, published in 1962, U.S. naturalist Rachel Carson alerted people to the deadly effects of chemicals such as DDT, sprayed on crops and entering the food chain. The theory of the greenhouse effect, saying that pollution was causing global warming, was first proposed in the 1960s.

There was growing concern about using up fossil fuels such as coal and oil. But the 1960s was still a time of technological optimism, when most people believed that science would find ready answers to such problems. Most advanced countries had large programs for building nuclear power plants. It was argued that nuclear power would provide a clean, inexhaustible source of energy to replace fossil fuels. This was to prove one of the most over-optimistic of all the 1960s attitudes.

Rachel Carson wrote:

"What we have to face is not an occasional dose of poison which has accidentally got into some article of food, but a persistent and continuous poisoning of the whole human environment."

▷ *A protective suit for nuclear power station workers, 1964*

A LOOK AT
FASHION
IN THE '60s

The 1960s was the decade when the focus of fashion became what young people were wearing on the street, rather than what was exhibited in haute-couture fashion shows. Also, men became much more style-conscious, where fashion previously had been seen as mostly a woman's concern.

△ *Customers at a restaurant in 1963 listen to and watch a new-style jukebox showing moving pictures of the singers.*

The early 1960s look

Fashions changed a lot in the course of the 1960s. In the early part of the decade, the cool look for men was sharp suits with narrow bottoms to the leg (sometimes called "drainpipe trousers"). Women tottered along on high "stiletto" heels, and many wore their hair up in "beehive" styles. Together the hair and heels made them look taller than they were.

The dresses women wore were designed to emphasize the curves of their hips and busts. Underneath they wore stockings and suspenders and forcefully uplifting bras. The ideal body shape was thought to be the full figure of the popular fifties sex symbol, Marilyn Monroe.

Swinging London

In the mid-1960s, the "in" look changed radically. There was a fashion revolution that started in London. A group of talented people, including fashion designers Mary Quant and John Stephen, hairdresser

" "

Mary Quant said:

"I wanted everyone to retain the grace of a child and not to have to become stilted, confined, ugly beings. So I created clothes that worked and moved and allowed people to run, to jump, to leap, to retain their precious freedom."

◁ *Minidress and matching-colored pantyhose designed by Mary Quant*

...Newsflash...

April 15, 1966. The United States has discovered the new London of youth and fun. The current edition of the news magazine *Time* has made "Swinging London" the subject of its cover story. Most Americans still think of Great Britain as a conservative place, associated with the Empire and bowler hats. But *Time* reveals that London has become the fashion center of the world. The magazine writes: "In this century, every decade has its city ... and for the Sixties that city is London."

John V. Lindsay, the mayor of New York City, was a typical man of his time in his response to the miniskirt. He said, jocularly:

"It will enable girls to run faster, and because of it, they may have to!"

▽ *Shoppers on London's Carnaby Street, the center of 1960s young fashion*

hairdresser Vidal Sassoon, and photographer David Bailey, made "Swinging London" the fashion capital of the world. Swinging London generated new fashions that were meant to be fun and were aimed specifically at young people.

The new look

The single most striking feature of the new look was the miniskirt, and Mary Quant is remembered as the designer most responsible for it. For the first time, women showed their thighs in public. Pantyhose were introduced to replace stockings, because stockings were too revealing under the very short hemlines.

Leading London models such as Jean Shrimpton and Twiggy made fashionable the skinny look, with no visible waist or bust. Women wore their hair long and straight with bangs or cut short in one of the striking geometrical looks pioneered by Vidal Sassoon.

Designers experimented with fun new materials such as vinyl and PVC, making shiny wet-look raincoats.

As women's skirts got shorter, young men's hair grew longer. Collarless Beatles jackets were the height of fashion. Wide ties came in, and the bottoms of men's trousers began to flare outward. Black polo-neck sweaters were fashionable, along with hip-huggers—jeans or trousers with the waistband at hip level.

▽ Vinyl was the look in Pierre Cardin's spring 1969 fashions. Here men model boots and zippered jackets.

◁ Jean Shrimpton caused a scandal when she attended a sports event in Australia in 1965 in a minidress and with no hat, gloves, or stockings.

Style wars

Jeans and T-shirts, associated before with manual workers, became the basic clothing of young people across the world. This was part of a general revolt against formality. Many young men rejected suits and ties as too stuffy and conventional.

Earlier fashions had been designed to make men and women look different. But from the mid-1960s, many fashions were "unisex." With some women having short hair, and some men long hair, and both sexes wearing hip-huggers and T-shirts, it was often quite difficult to tell the sexes apart. Many older people found this very disturbing.

Although the new fashions originated in England, France quickly developed its own style for the sixties. Designer André Courrèges made an impact with his futuristic "Space Age" collection, which featured his "moon girl" look. This design reflected the current enthusiasm for space exploration. Like Courrèges, many other

Profile

Twiggy

Sixties model Twiggy (real name Lesley Hornby) was born in a London suburb in 1949. She was rejected by modeling schools because she was too short and her hips were too narrow. But this setback was short-lived, because she was still only 16 when the London press discovered her as "the face of 1966." She soon made a triumphant visit to the United States, where her youthful charm, startling figure, and ultramodish short haircut caused a sensation. Twiggy remained a fashionable figure into the 1970s.

French designers began experimenting with new materials. Paco Rabanne designed what he called a "chain mail" evening dress, made of mylar. Yves Saint Laurent, who had started his own fashion house in 1962, designed "pop art" dresses inspired by the likes of Andy Warhol and Dutch artist Piet Mondrian. Pierre Cardin's unisex styles continued the trend of girls looking like boys and vice versa.

▷ *Pants suits modeled in London, 1967*

△ *Yves Saint Laurent's "pop-art" dress*

Afghans and Afros

Toward the end of the 1960s, more shifts in style took place. The spreading influence of the Hippie movement led to the wearing of embroidered blouses, Afghan coats, ethnic skirts, beads, and even cowbells. Young men's hair became even longer, and beards and mustaches grew in popularity. But the decade-long trend toward shorter hemlines stopped. Medium-length "midiskirts" and ankle-length "maxiskirts" came in alongside the mini. Some women wore long maxicoats over miniskirts.

◁ *Tie-dyed trousers and an Afghan vest at an open-air festival, 1967*

▷ *Dancing at a Los Angeles club. This woman's body is painted with psyche-delic designs under a plastic dress.*

For African Americans, the 1960s also marked a style revolution, though of a different kind. At the start of the decade, most African Americans liked to be as fair as possible—that is, pale rather than dark-skinned. They also used to straighten their hair, taking out the kink natural to African hair. But the "black is beautiful" slogan of the second half of the 1960s led many African Americans to change their attitude about their looks. The more radical adopted Afro hairstyles designed to emphasize their ethnic origins. Some also wore African-style brightly patterned fabrics.

Without going that far, most African Americans were influenced by the trend to take pride in their ethnic identity.

◁ *An Afro hairstyle*

A LOOK AT
MUSIC
IN THE '60s

Most music fans look back on the 1960s as a golden age of rock. Heroes of the decade, such as the Beatles, Bob Dylan, Jimi Hendrix, and Jim Morrison, are still revered by many. Such gifted individuals gave rock music a new status as a key element in modern cultural life that continues today.

▽ *Young people study album covers in a record store in 1965.*

A large youth market for records had developed for the first time in the 1950s, as young people came to have more spending money. The recording business grew phenomenally in the 1960s. By 1967, record sales in the United States were worth more than $1 billion a year. This was more than double the value of record sales ten years earlier.

The records were all shiny vinyl discs. (Cassettes only began to come in at the very end of the decade.) Records were often released in two versions, mono and stereo. Early in the decade, only a minority of people had stereo equipment. The sound quality available to most listeners was quite poor.

Good-bye
sock hops;
Buddy Holly

Hello
Pop festivals;
light shows;
Beatlemania;
Motown

Their record players had small built-in speakers, and the records gathered dust and got scratched. Yet listening through the crackle and hiss of the needle finding its way along the grooves of the record, young people found amazing excitement in the fresh new music that was being made.

Profile

Joan Baez

Joan Baez, seen here with Bob Dylan, with whom she was closely associated, was a leading figure on the folk scene in the 1960s. Her beautiful voice won her a huge following, with songs such as "What Have They Done to the Rain?" The daughter of a Mexican-American scientist, she was a dedicated campaigner against racism and U.S. involvement in Vietnam. She was twice jailed for her anti-war protests, when she joined demonstrators blocking the way into induction centers, where young Americans were sent to join the army.

Motown and folk

At the start of the 1960s, pop was at a low point. The rock 'n' roll boom of the 1950s, led by Elvis Presley and Bill Haley, had run out of steam. But in Detroit, a former boxer, Berry Gordy, Jr, launched the Motown label in 1960. With performers such as Diana Ross (of the Supremes), Stevie Wonder, and Marvin Gaye, Motown was soon turning out a string of hits that became the top dance music of the decade.

Another strand in the creation of the 1960s music scene was the folk music of singer-songwriters such as Bob Dylan and Joan Baez. In the early 1960s, they performed songs you couldn't dance to—accompanied by acoustic guitar—to quiet, respectful white audiences in New York City or at annual folk festivals across the country. But by 1965 folk had gone hip. Braving the hostility of his dedicated folk fans, Dylan got an electric backup band and produced songs that were closer to the rock music of the Rolling Stones.

▽ *The Supremes. Diana Ross is on the left.*

Rule Britannia

The main influence that turned Bob Dylan electric was the incredible popularity of British rock music. Until 1963, most British music had been a weak imitation of Elvis Presley and Little Richard. But British youth culture was beginning to bubble with fresh ideas. In 1962, a well-established Liverpool band, the Beatles, recorded their first national hit single, "Love Me Do." Within a year, "Beatlemania" had swept Great Britain. In scenes of mass hysteria, crowds of screaming teenagers mobbed the "Moptops" wherever they went. In 1964, the Beatles went on a tour of the United States and received a similar welcome there.

The Beatles arrive in the United States, 1964. ▷

...Newsflash...

February 9, 1964. Britain's top pop group, the Beatles, have arrived in the United States and are taking the country by storm. When the Fab Four touched down at New York's Kennedy Airport two days ago, thousands of screaming fans had turned up to give them a big welcome. Their song "I Want to Hold Your Hand" is already top of the Hot 100 singles chart, and their appearance on *The Ed Sullivan Show* tonight has drawn a record TV audience of 73 million. For the first time, Americans are rocking to a British beat.

" "

According to Beatle Paul McCartney, the Beatles themselves were often shocked at how seriously people took them. Of fans who blamed the Beatles for failing to change the world, he said:

"I don't really think that we thought that we were going to change the world as much as you thought we were going to change the world."

In the wake of the Beatles, a series of British bands stormed the pop charts on both sides of the Atlantic: the Rolling Stones, Gerry and the Pacemakers, the Kinks, the Animals, and the Who. The Beatles themselves split up in 1970 to pursue solo careers. The U.S. entertainment industry paid them the compliment of imitation, manufacturing a band, the Monkees, modeled on the Beatles, for a TV series.

△ *The Kinks, 1968*

Profile

Jimi Hendrix

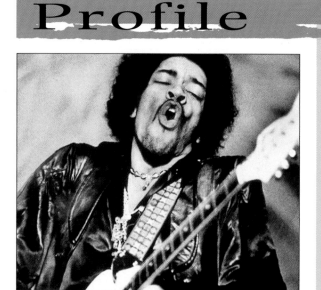

Born in Seattle, Washington, Jimi Hendrix was a paratrooper in the U.S. Army before making his living as a musician. In 1967 he shot to fame after appearing at the Monterey Pop Festival with his band, the Jimi Hendrix Experience. He was a guitar player of genius, who constantly experimented with imaginative new sounds. He also developed a wild stage act that sometimes ended with him setting his guitar on fire. He died in London in September 1970, two months before his 28th birthday.

Voices of a generation

The new British sound was fresh, irreverent, and fun. But 1960s rock music soon began to get heavier. The influences of the Hippie drug culture and of youth protest began to be felt. Rock stars became conscious of being the "voice of a generation," often at odds with the authorities. They wrote their own material, creating lyrics that were far removed from the simple love songs of most previous pop music.

Unusual instruments such as the sitar appeared on rock records, as did strange electronic effects. Bands such as Cream and the Jimi Hendrix Experience explored the potential of the electric guitar to the limits in often rambling solos. The Beatles' 1967 album *Sergeant Pepper's Lonely Hearts Club Band* started a new tradition of concept albums—linked tracks instead of a collection of singles.

△ *Listening to one of the bands at Woodstock, 1969*

Festival time

In 1967 the era of open-air festivals began. It reached its peak with the Woodstock festival in 1969. Events such as Woodstock were given a great deal of press. Listening to bands such as

1960s rock festivals were almost all badly organized, with poor facilities and inadequate sound systems.
John Leaver, who worked on an underground magazine, remembers:

"I'm sitting in the middle of a field with 50,000 other people and the Grateful Dead are half a mile away, and I'm thinking, 'I must be having fun.'"

...Newsflash...

Bethel, August 17, 1969. Some 400,000 young people have swarmed to the small town of Bethel in New York State for the Woodstock Music and Arts Fair. They have been drawn by a list of performers that includes Jefferson Airplane, the Who, Janis Joplin, and Crosby, Stills, Nash, and Young. The weekend is being hailed as a triumphant celebration of youth culture. Despite traffic jams, shortages of food and water, and torrential rain, everyone seems to be having a good time.

Jefferson Airplane, the Grateful Dead, and the Doors, the young generation was supposed to experience itself as a "counterculture" of peace and love, opposed to the money-obsessed, war-making culture of its parents. But for some who went, it was just a fun way of passing a weekend.

▽ *The Grateful Dead, Woodstock, 1969*

A LOOK AT
ART and ARCHITECTURE
IN THE '60s

In the 1960s many painters and sculptors wanted to take part in the fun and glamor of popular culture. They created a new movement called pop art, which was up-to-date, witty, and accessible.

Pop art

Pop art drew much of its inspiration from advertising, supermarket goods, movies, and comic books. It first hit the headlines in 1962, when American artist Andy Warhol exhibited reproductions of Campbell's soup cans. Warhol's other works included repeated images of pop idols such as Elvis Presley and Marilyn Monroe. Other American pop artists included Roy Lichtenstein and Claes Oldenburg.

Pop art also flourished in Great Britain, with artists such as David Hockney and Richard Hamilton. In the second half of the 1960s, Hockney moved to California, where he made a famous series of paintings of swimming pools.

Pop art marked a real change in the attitude of the art world. Artists began to take popular culture seriously, and to take themselves less seriously. British pop artist Richard Hamilton said his art was

"popular, transient, expendable, low-cost, mass-produced, young, witty, sexy, gimmicky, glamorous, and Big Business."

▽ Roy Lichtenstein made art, such as "Whaam!" (1963), out of blown-up images from comic strips. It is said that he was first inspired by one of his children who pointed to a comic book and said, "I bet you can't paint as good as that!"

Profile

Andy Warhol

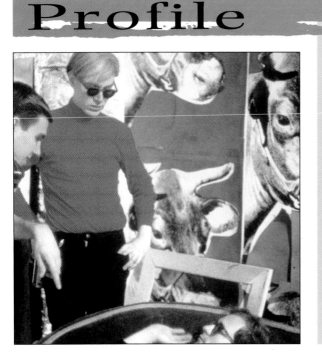

Pop artist Andy Warhol caused a sensation in 1962 when he exhibited pictures of Campbell's soup cans in an art gallery.
He called his New York studio "The Factory" and set out to mass-produce art, as factories mass-produced identical consumer goods.

Warhol also made strange movies—one of them, called *Sleep*, showed a man sleeping for five and a half hours—and promoted a rock group, the Velvet Underground. In 1968 he was shot and seriously wounded by Valerie Solanas, founder of the Society for Cutting Up Men (SCUM). Warhol died in 1987.

△ *Andy Warhol, in red, and friends in his studio*

▽ *Swedish-born American artist Claes Oldenburg produced giant sculptures of food, such as ice-cream cones and hamburgers and "soft sculptures" of normally hard objects, like this "Soft Drum Kit" of 1967. It is made of vinyl and canvas, filled with expanded polystyrene chips.*

Even artists who were not part of the pop art movement often reacted to the sense of color and modernity bursting into 1960s life. In Great Britain, for example, sculpture was dominated at first by the somber bronze sculptures of Henry Moore, based on natural forms. But Moore's influence waned in the 1960s, and the rising star was Anthony Caro, who produced sculptures in bright colors, using manufactured materials such as aluminum tubes and steel plates. Caro said he wanted to produce sculptures that had absolutely nothing to do with the art of the past.

Making it happen

Another feature of 1960s art was the "happening."
This was a bizarre or provocative event presented
as a work of art. French artist Yves Klein, for
example, "conducted" naked women who
smeared each other with paint, while an
orchestra played and a formally dressed
audience looked on. Another artist who
created happenings was Yoko Ono, who later
married Beatle John Lennon. On one
occasion she sat on stage, and members of the
audience were invited to come up to cut off
pieces of her dress with scissors.

Yoko Ono's involvement with the Beatles was one
example of how the world of art crossed
over with pop music and fashion in the 1960s.
Andy Warhol promoted the Velvet Underground,
featuring singer Lou Reed. By 1965 the Beatles were mixing
in the arty world of Swinging London, a setting far removed
from the seedy nightclubs they had begun their careers in. The cover
for the Beatles' *Sergeant Pepper's Lonely Hearts Club Band* album was
designed by pop artist Peter Blake.

△ *An op art dress by an
Italian designer is modeled
in Milan in 1966.*

Mary Quant and other
fashion designers
produced a range of
black-and-white clothes
based on op art. This
was an art movement
exploiting visual
illusions created by
strange abstract
patterns.

◁ *The Beatles' Bentley
was painted with
psychedelic designs.*

Building styles

Most 1960s architecture was in the "modernist" style that had triumphed across the globe since the end of World War II. In almost every city and every country, high-rise concrete and glass buildings were going up, designed in a functional style that avoided fussy details or anything that might recall the architecture of the past. Tall buildings transformed skylines in previously low-rise cities.

Ordinary people always had problems with this style of architecture, especially when they were asked to live in high-rise buildings or housing projects. The era of this international style was coming to an end. It would not be long before the authorities started knocking down these buildings, and architects began designing unusual buildings that were fun again.

R. Buckminster Fuller was a famous and influential architect of the '60s. Like many architects and artists of the time, Fuller was inspired by the advances being made in the sciences. He decided to design a building based on the structure of organic compounds. Fuller's goal was a building of maximum strength with minimal structures. Using the simple three dimensional shapes of the four-sided tetrahedron and the eight-sided octahedron, Fuller developed the geodesic dome. It was constructed as the United States Exhibition dome for Expo 67 in Montreal, Quebec. This design has since been widely used around the world.

Nigel Waymouth designed psychedelic posters in the 1960s. He later explained:

"Before that fly-posters were very dull. ... We decided to paint pictures and use the gaudiest and the brightest colours, rainbow colours, silver, gold .... It was great fun and it brightened up all those [shabby] corrugated iron fences."

▽ Buckminster Fuller's geodesic dome in Montreal, 1967

Psychedelia

In the second half of the 1960s, youth culture produced its own art style, known as psychedelia. American artist Milton Glaser was the finest exponent of psychedelic posters and album covers in the later 1960s. With its bright colors and swirly patterns, psychedelia was supposed to represent mind-altering drug experiences.

A LOOK AT

SPORTS

IN THE '60s

▽ *Abebe Bikila, from Ethiopia, won the marathon at the Olympic Games in Rome, 1960. He ran the race barefoot.*

In the 1960s sports became more commercial. They also became more involved with political issues, especially the question of equal rights for black people. But what really mattered for sports fans, as usual, were the outstanding performances of supremely talented individuals.

When the 1960s began, there were still sports where the ideal of amateurism was upheld—the principle that people should not earn money from their sport. The Wimbledon tennis tournament, for example, was only open to amateur players. But more and more of the

Profile

Muhammad Ali

Possibly the greatest boxer of all time, Muhammad Ali first made his mark as an amateur, winning a gold medal at the 1960 Rome Olympics. At that time he was known as Cassius Clay. He changed his name to Muhammad Ali after joining the black Muslim movement, the Nation of Islam, in 1964. In the same year, he became world heavyweight champion. Ali had his title taken away in 1967 after he refused to serve in the U.S. Army in protest against the Vietnam war. He won the title back twice in the 1970s.

◁ *November 1965: Muhammad Ali (left) in a match with Floyd Patterson.*

...Newsflash...

Mexico City, October 1968.
American 200-meter gold medalist Tommie Smith and bronze winner John Carlos have been suspended from the Olympics and thrown out of the Olympic village after a sensational demonstration in favor of black rights in the United States. U.S. athletics officials were stunned as the pair bowed their heads and raised black-gloved fists in the Black Power salute after receiving their medals. It was a deliberate gesture of solidarity with African Americans fighting against what they see as oppression and racism in the United States. The authorities have made it clear that the two athletes will be made to pay dearly for their political gesture.

△ *Having received their medals at the Mexico Olympics, African-American athletes Tommie Smith and John Carlos gave Black Power salutes while the U.S. national anthem was played. For doing so they were banned from the American team.*

top tennis stars became professionals, and consequently could not play at Wimbledon. In 1968, the International Lawn Tennis Association was forced to abolish the distinction between amateurs and professionals, opening Wimbledon to all.

In sports that had long been big business, such as major-league baseball and soccer, the star players began to take a larger cut of the profits. In 1960, top British soccer players earned little more than an average workingman. By the end of the decade, stars such as Manchester United's George Best had become wealthy high earners. Football set out to increase its profits by starting the Super Bowl in 1967.

Race and sports

The question of black rights was bound to have an impact on sports because so many top performers were black. South Africa's racist policies led to a movement for the country to be banned from world sports. The climax came when the South Africans themselves refused to compete against nonwhites.

In the United States, sports personalities such as boxer Cassius Clay (Muhammad Ali) and athletes Tommie Smith and John Carlos became involved in the struggle for black rights.

ENGLAND 3 GERMANY W. 2

◁ In the 1966 World Cup final between England and Germany, Geoff Hurst (right) shoots to score the fourth goal for England.

For the English, the greatest sports event of the decade was England's soccer team winning the World Cup at Wembley in 1966.

Americans dominated golf. Arnold Palmer was the leading golfer at the start of the decade, but in 1962 another young American, Jack Nicklaus, won his first major tournament. By the end of the decade, Nicklaus was well on his way to becoming the most successful golfer of all time.

At the Rome Olympics in 1960, Ethiopian Abebe Bikila astonished the crowds by winning the marathon—barefoot. He won again at the Tokyo Olympics in 1964—the first person to gain two consecutive marathon golds. The Mexico Olympics in 1968 produced some outstanding records, partly because the games were held at high altitude, aiding performances.

Known as the Golden Bear because he was "large, strong, blond, and maybe a little growly," Jack Nicklaus wrote that:

"In golf, almost everyone loses a whole lot more than he wins .... The most obvious reason is surely the huge role luck plays in golf."

▷ Carrying the Olympic flame at the Tokyo Olympics in 1964 was student Yoshinori Sakai. He was born on August 6, 1945, the day that the atomic bomb was dropped on the Japanese city of Hiroshima.

Profile

Billie Jean King

Born in California in 1943, Billie Jean King (born Billie Jean Moffitt) became famous in the 1960s as the top woman tennis star of her generation. She won her first Wimbledon women's singles title in 1966, beating Maria Bueno in the final, and retained the title for the next two years.

King's powerful, aggressive style of play challenged the assumption that men's tennis was better than women's. She remained a leading player throughout the 1970s, winning the Wimbledon singles title three more times.

△ *Billie Jean King (then Billie Jean Moffitt), June 1962*

American athlete Bob Beamon broke the world long jump record by 21 in. (55 cm), setting a record that lasted until 1991. Another American athlete, Dick Fosbury, won the high jump gold with a revolutionary style of jump, known as the Fosbury Flop.

Australians excelled in tennis, with Rod Laver the leading male player and Margaret Court the leading female star. However, Court's dominance was challenged in the later 1960s by the young American Billie Jean King.

A LOOK AT
LEISURE and ENTERTAINMENT
IN THE '60s

In the 1960s watching television was by far the most popular leisure activity. It was still a relatively novel experience, since television broadcasting had not really been established until the 1950s. There were fewer TV channels than there are today, and most people had only small black-and-white TV sets. But the poor picture quality and limited choice of programs did not lessen viewers' enjoyment.

Families gathered around their TVs to watch Westerns such as *Rawhide* and *Bonanza*, suspense series such as *The Man from U.N.C.L.E.*, *The Avengers*, and *The Fugitive*, and science-fiction series *Star Trek* and *Dr. Who*. Popular comedies included *The Addams Family*, *The Munsters*, *The Beverly Hillbillies*, and *Bewitched*.

Hello

The Avengers, Twilight Zone, Route 66, 1960; The Flintstones, 1961; Dr. Who, 1963; The Outer Limits, Flipper, 1964; Get Smart, 1965; Star Trek, Mission Impossible, 1966; The Smothers Brothers Comedy Hour, 1967; Monty Python's Flying Circus, 1969

▽ In "The Fugitive," a character called Dr. Richard Kimble was on the run from a policeman, after the murder of his wife, and always chasing the real murderer—the one-armed man shown here.

The steamy soap opera *Peyton Place* starred future movie stars Mia Farrow and Ryan O'Neal. News magazine TV shows became immensely popular. *Sixty Minutes* began in 1968 and is still flourishing.

The irreverent side of the 1960s was represented by programs such as the *Smothers Brothers Comedy Hour* and the zany comedy show *Rowan and Martin's Laugh-In*, which made Goldie Hawn a star. One of its catch phrases was "Sock it to me!"

The poet and critic T.S. Eliot wrote in the *New York Post* in September 1963 that television

"permits millions of people to listen to the same joke at the same time, and yet remain lonesome."

▷ *Goldie Hawn and Sammy Davis Jr. on the set of the comedy show, "Rowan and Martin's Laugh-In" in October 1968.*

Television also brought events of the day into people's homes with a new vividness. During the Vietnam War, people saw images of death and destruction on their TV sets every evening. Only 20 years earlier, during World War II, people had had to rely on newspaper reports and photos and movie newsreels.

▽ *The Monkees (left to right: Davy Jones, Micky Dolenz, Peter Tork, and Mike Nesmith) were formed especially for a TV series, full of zany action.*

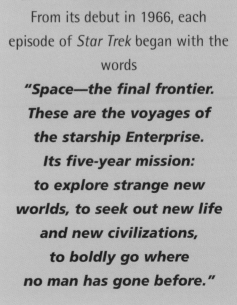

From its debut in 1966, each episode of *Star Trek* began with the words
"Space—the final frontier. These are the voyages of the starship Enterprise. Its five-year mission: to explore strange new worlds, to seek out new life and new civilizations, to boldly go where no man has gone before."

At the movies

At the start of the 1960s, the movie industry was in crisis because it was losing customers to television. The movie companies tried to attract people away from their black-and-white TV sets by presenting lavish visual spectacles, making wide-screen epics such as *Cleopatra, Lawrence of Arabia,* and *Dr. Zhivago.* Later in the decade, Hollywood began to lure audiences with movies that had a degree of explicit sex and violence in them that was beyond anything allowed on television.

Westerns were big in the 1960s, from *The Magnificent Seven* in 1960 to the violent Italian-made "spaghetti Westerns" such as *A Fistful of Dollars,* starring Clint Eastwood, and the comedy Western *Butch Cassidy and the Sundance Kid,* starring Paul Newman and Robert Redford, in 1969.

▽ *In* Butch Cassidy and the Sundance Kid, *American society is seen from the outlaw's point of view.*

Profile

Sidney Poitier

Sometimes described as the first black superstar, Sidney Poitier was called upon whenever the movies needed a worthy, charming, courageous African American. In 1964 he became the first black performer to win an Academy Award for best actor, for his role in *Lilies of the Field.* His most memorable film role was as a sophisticated black detective, Virgil Tibbs, in the 1967 film *In the Heat of the Night.* Set in a small town in Mississippi, the film is a powerful study of racial prejudice.

Profile

Julie Christie

Born in 1940, British actress Julie Christie had her first starring role in the film *Billy Liar* in 1963. She was soon seen as someone who typically represented the spirit of Swinging London, with its miniskirts and liberated young women. In 1965 she won an Academy Award for her part as a spoiled model in *Darling*. Christie went on to star in other successful movies, including *Dr. Zhivago*, where she played opposite a heartthrob of the period, Omar Sharif, and *Far from the Madding Crowd*.

◁ *Christie in the 1966 movie* Fahrenheit 451

Special effects made great strides in Stanley Kubrick's science-fiction movie *2001: A Space Odyssey*. Disney feature-length cartoons included *The Jungle Book*, the first Disney cartoon to have a pop music soundtrack.

▽ *Julie Andrews sings "My Favorite Things" in the 1965 movie version of* The Sound of Music.

James Bond movies, starring Sean Connery, were immensely successful. The first was *Dr. No* in 1962, followed by *From Russia with Love* in 1963. Julie Andrews was a hit in the musicals *The Sound of Music* and *Mary Poppins*. Comedian Peter Sellars starred in *Dr. Strangelove* and the Pink Panther movies. The Beatles made their own cartoon feature film, *Yellow Submarine*, as well as starring in *A Hard Day's Night* and *Help!*

Throughout the 1960s, censorship became steadily less heavy-handed. Many older people complained about the increasing amount of explicit sex and foul language found on television and in the movies. Yet even by the end of the decade, there was nothing like as much nudity or obscenity allowed on screens as we are used to today.

Dance

Dance crazes came and went through the decade. The most famous of them was the Twist, introduced by singer Chubby Checker in 1960. As the decade progressed, dancing became less structured, with more free self-expression. Discos were livened up with rather primitive psychedelic light shows and strobes.

▷ Americans danced the Twist everywhere—even on beaches.

Other youth activities

In the early 1960s, the coolest youth activities in the United States were driving hot rods—souped-up secondhand cars—and surfing. But the influence of the Hippie revolution made young people more laid back. Throwing a frisbee was the coolest late-1960s cult, because it was seen as noncompetitive and peaceful, ideal for spaced-out afternoons in the park.

Open-air music festivals became larger and more frequent as the decade went on, culminating in the famous Woodstock festival in 1969. These events were good opportunities for young people to explore sexual experiences and experiment with "consciousness-expanding" drugs such as LSD (or "acid").

Amsterdam and Copenhagen became popular vacation destinations for the young, because of tolerant attitudes there toward drugs. Thousands of young people also followed the "Hippie trail"—the long overland route from Europe to Afghanistan and India.

Travel

Most young people either hitchhiked or traveled by bus or train. Although young Americans could afford transatlantic flights to see Europe, traveling by air was simply too expensive for most students. Yet air travel was becoming increasingly available to ordinary people. Vacation spots in the Caribbean and in Europe became easier and quicker to get to, and many new resorts grew up around the world.

Childhood in the 1960s

For children, there were, compared with today, few interesting things to do in the 1960s. Go-karting was a craze of the time. Slot cars, with electric racing cars guided around a track by handheld controls, were the most hi-tech toys available.

Lego, invented in the 1950s, was becoming popular, although in a primitive form with little more than rectangular blocks in different colors. Barbie dolls and Action Man toys both became popular for the first time in the 1960s. Primitive skateboards—flat wooden boards pedaled along with the free foot like a scooter—had existed for a decade in the United States but were little used. For many children, their most prized possession was a bicycle—ridden without a crash helmet. In the absence of videotapes, video games, home computers, and theme parks, the revolution in childhood was still to happen.

▽ *The start of a 20-lap go-kart race*

▽ *On the "Hippie trail" in Kathmandu, Nepal*

A student describes an overseas vacation in 1968:

"I set off to hitchhike around Europe with a small backpack, a sleeping bag, and $80 for six weeks. Hitchhiking could be tough. Because of my long hair, lots of drivers were aggressive, shouted things or made signs. But I met other young people like myself, slept on beaches and in parks, had adventures. And I arrived back home with 35¢ in my pocket."

Date List

1960

February 3 ▷ British prime minister Harold Macmillan makes a speech declaring that "the wind of change is blowing through Africa." Great Britain, France, and Belgium all begin a rapid withdrawal from their African colonies.

May 1 ▷ An American U2 spy plane piloted by Gary Powers is shot down over the Soviet Union.

June ▷ The Motown record label is launched in Detroit.

August ▷ The Twist emerges as the biggest dance craze for many years.

October 1 ▷ Great Britain grants independence to Nigeria. Great Britain's other African colonies become independent over the following five years.

November 8 ▷ John F. Kennedy wins the presidential election. Aged 43, he is the youngest ever American president.

Also in 1960 ... ▷ The U.S. Food and Drug Administration approves the birth control pill for sale in the United States.

1961

April 12 ▷ Soviet cosmonaut Yuri Gagarin becomes the first man in space, orbiting the earth on a 108-minute flight.

August 13 ▷ Berlin is divided in two as the building of a wall begins that separates communist East Berlin from West Berlin.

1962

February 20 ▷ John Glenn becomes the first American to orbit the earth.

October 22 ▷ The Cuban missile crisis begins when President Kennedy announces that the Soviet Union is stationing nuclear missiles in Cuba. The crisis eventually ends with the dismantling of the Soviet missile sites.

July 10 ▷ The communications satellite Telstar is launched. It allows the first broadcast of television pictures across the Atlantic.

October 31 ▷ Pop art hits the headlines as a major exhibition opens in New York, including Andy Warhol's pictures of Campbell's soup cans.

Also in 1962 ... ▷ Rachel Carson publishes *Silent Spring*, pointing out the dangers of the use of pesticides in farming.

1963

May ▷ The Beatles release their first album, *Please Please Me*.

June 5 ▷ British defense minister John Profumo is forced to resign after a scandal involving call girl Christine Keeler.

August 28 ▷ More than 200,000 people, led by Martin Luther King, Jr., demonstrate for Civil Rights in the March on Washington.

November 22 ▷ President Kennedy is assassinated in Dallas, Texas.

Also in 1963 ... ▷ Betty Friedan publishes *The Feminine Mystique*, seen as the starting point of the Women's Movement.

1964

February 7 ▷ The Beatles begin their triumphant first visit to the United States.

February 25 ▷ Cassius Clay (Muhammad Ali) defeats Sonny Liston to become world heavyweight boxing champion.

June 14 ▷ South African anti-apartheid leader Nelson Mandela is sentenced to life imprisonment for treason.

1965

March 8 ▷ U.S. combat troops are sent into South Vietnam to fight communist guerrillas.

March 18 ▷ Soviet cosmonaut Alexei Leonov makes the first space walk.

Also in 1965 ... ▷ The miniskirt, first sold in Mary Quant's London boutique, takes the fashion world by storm.

1966

April ▷ *Time* magazine declares that the grooviest city in the world is "Swinging London."

May ▷ Mass parades of young Red Guards march through Peking as China's Cultural Revolution gets under way.

July 2 ▷ Billie Jean King wins her first Wimbledon singles title.

July 30 ▷ England's soccer team wins the World Cup at Wembley, beating West Germany 4–2 after extra time.

Also in 1966 ... ▷ The sci-fi series *Star Trek* appears for the first time on U.S. television.

1967

January 15 ▷ Football's first Superbowl is won by the Green Bay Packers.

March 19 ▷ An oil tanker, the *Torrey Canyon*, runs onto rocks off Cornwall, spilling vast quantities of crude oil into the sea.

June 1 ▷ The Beatles' concept album *Sergeant Pepper's Lonely Hearts Club Band* is released.

June 5–10 ▷ Israel defeats its Arab neighbors in the Six-Day War.

June 18 ▷ Jimi Hendrix achieves stardom at the open-air Monterey Pop Festival.

October 10 ▷ The body of Latin American revolutionary leader Che Guevara is displayed to the world's press. He was killed trying to start an uprising in Bolivia.

December 3 ▷ The world's first successful heart transplant operation is carried out by Dr. Christiaan Barnard in Cape Town, South Africa.

1968

April 4 ▷ Civil Rights leader Martin Luther King, Jr., is assassinated at a motel in Memphis, Tennessee.

May 10 ▷ Students battle with police in Paris on the "Night of the Barricades." The riots spark a student revolt and general strike that bring France to a halt for a month.

June 5 ▷ Robert Kennedy, younger brother of the late President John F. Kennedy, is shot dead by a Palestinian, Sirhan Sirhan.

August 21 ▷ The Soviet Union and some of its allies invade Czechoslovakia to end the experiment with liberal communism known as the Prague Spring.

October ▷ The Olympic Games are held in Mexico. American sprinters Tommie Smith and John Carlos are expelled for giving the Black Power salute.

1969

July 20 ▷ Neil Armstrong is the first person to set foot on the moon in the successful *Apollo 11* mission.

August 14 ▷ British troops are sent onto the streets of Northern Ireland to restore order after violence flares up between Protestants and Catholics.

August 17 ▷ The Woodstock festival ends after three days of music by Jefferson Airplane, Janis Joplin, the Who, Jimi Hendrix, and many others.

Glossary

ANC

ANC stands for African National Congress, the organization that led the resistance to apartheid in South Africa. After 1994, the ANC became the leading party in the postapartheid South African government.

apartheid

Apartheid was the system of racial segregation operated by the white rulers of South Africa between 1949 and 1992.

Black Power

Black Power was a loosely structured movement that developed among African Americans in the second half of the 1960s. It suggested that black people should assert their own values rather than seeking integration in white society. Black Power radicals also believed that the use of force was often justified, especially in self-defense.

boutique

A small shop selling fashionable clothes.

capital punishment

The punishment of a crime by death.

Carnaby Street

A street in London's West End where many clothing stores for young people were opened in the 1960s.

CIA

CIA stands for the Central Intelligence Agency, the U.S. organization responsible for spying and other secret activities against America's enemies.

Cold War

The Cold War was the period of tension between the United States and its allies on one side, and the Soviet Union and its allies on the other. It lasted from the late 1940s to the late 1980s.

communism

Communism is a political and economic system that was first established in the Soviet Union and spread from there to many other countries. Under this system, a single party ruled without tolerating any opposition, and industry and agriculture were controlled by the state.

DDT

An insecticide known to cause long-term damage to animals and humans when used in farming.

flower power

The Hippie belief in changing the world through peace and love.

folk music

A type of music popular in the early 1960s, using an American folk song style to present lyrics protesting against war, nuclear weapons, and racial prejudice.

generation gap

The difference in attitudes, values, and behavior between adults and young people. The generation gap existed in acute form in the 1960s.

Hippie

Hippie is a term used for people in the 1960s who rejected conventional society because of its obsession with work and money. Hippies advocated peace and love and experimented with mind-altering drugs.

Iron Curtain

The Iron Curtain was a term used for the imaginary line that divided Western Europe from communist-controlled Eastern Europe from the late 1940s to the late 1980s.

KGB

Soviet secret police and spying organization.

Motown

African-American record label based in the car-making city of Detroit. The name was derived from Detroit's nickname, Motor Town.

Nation of Islam

African-American movement preaching the Islamic religion and promoting specifically black values against white society.

NATO

NATO stands for the North Atlantic Treaty Organization, an alliance set up in 1949 by the United States and its West European allies to oppose the power of the Soviet Union.

Prague Spring

An attempt in early 1968 to create a liberal form of communism in Czechoslovakia.

psychedelic

A term used for drugs such as LSD that produce hallucinations or altered visual perceptions. The use of the word was extended to refer to painting and clothing design using swirly, brightly colored patterns.

PVC

PVC stands for polyvinyl chloride, a kind of plastic.

satire

The use of humor to ridicule politicians and to criticize social customs or attitudes.

spaghetti Western

A term used for movies about American cowboys that were made in Europe by Italian filmmakers. Spaghetti Westerns were hugely popular in the 1960s, beginning with Sergio Leone's *A Fistful of Dollars* (1964), which starred Clint Eastwood.

Summer of Love

A name given to the summer of 1967, because of the huge number of Hippie-influenced open-air festivals, Be-Ins, and Love-Ins that were held then.

Resources

Books

One good place to start reading on the 1960s is Jonathon Green's *Days in the Life* (Heinemann-Mandarin, 1988), a series of fascinating snippets from interviews with hundreds of people, both famous and unknown, who were part of the London scene.

Or try Ian MacDonald's *Revolution in the Head* (New York: Henry Holt, 1995), an attempt to understand the new thinking of youth in the 1960s through Beatles' lyrics.

Among novels that help grasp what the 1960s were about, *One Flew Over the Cuckoo's Nest* by Ken Kesey stands out, with its vision of society as a madhouse we need to escape from.

James Baldwin's *Another Country*, first published in 1963, gives one black's take on the 1960s.

In a lighter vein, 1960s spy stories such as John Le Carré's *The Spy Who Came in from the Cold* and Len Deighton's *Funeral in Berlin* give a good feel of the Cold War side of the decade.

Thomas Pynchon's *Vineland* is a recent attempt to describe being young and radical in the decade of protest.

Tom Wolfe's *The Electric Kool-Aid Acid Test* is a classic book about the '60s written in the '60s—it looks at the wildest side of the drug-taking West Coast scene.

An even more extreme, hyped-up view of the drug scene is provided by Hunter S. Thompson's *Fear and Loathing in Las Vegas* (1972), in which two drugged Hippies go on an outing.

Australian journalist Richard Neville has written an enjoyable retrospective view of London in the late 1960s, *Hippie Hippie Shake*.

The radical political scene of antiwar protest is brilliantly captured in Norman Mailer's two 1960s classics *The Armies of the Night* and *Miami Beach and the Siege of Chicago*.

A good memoir of the Civil Rights struggle is Mary King's *Freedom Song*.

For a short and reasonably balanced view of the fight for equal rights, try *The Civil Rights Movement: Struggle and Resistance* by William T. Martin Riches.

To look at the whole period, a real heavyweight study is *The Sixties* by British historian Arthur Marwick (New York: Oxford University Press, 1998)—a dauntingly big book, but interestingly written.

Movies

Sixties movies turn up all the time on television and are often worth watching.

Dr. Strangelove: or How I Learned to Stop Worrying and Love the Bomb is a classic of 1960s satire, antiwar protest, and nuclear paranoia.

What's New Pussycat?, a 1965 comedy, shows the '60s at their silliest and is packed with crazes of the time such as go-karts.

The Beatles' movies, especially *A Hard Day's Night*, are essential viewing for the decade.

If you want to understand what the 1960s did to attitudes, you could try comparing the 1960 John Wayne Western *The Alamo* with the 1969 *Butch Cassidy and the Sundance Kid*.

One of the biggest hits of the decade was *The Graduate* (1967). Starring a young Dustin Hoffman, and with a soundtrack by Simon and Garfunkel, it was the perfect generation gap movie.

Bonnie and Clyde, also made in 1967, was essentially a "youth revolt" movie, although it was set in the gangster era of the 1930s.

Films directly about the Hippie period include the disturbing road movie *Easy Rider* and *Alice's Restaurant*, both made in 1969.

There are two excellent documentary movies on rock festivals: the famous *Woodstock* and the less well-known *Gimme Shelter*, about the Rolling Stones concert at Altamont, California, in 1969, which ended in violence.

Music

Much of 1960s music is familiar to everyone. Listening to Beatles or Beach Boys records in date order gives a run-through of changing '60s cultural styles.

You may not have heard early Bob Dylan songs such as "A Hard Rain's Gonna Fall" or "It's Alright Ma," a protest against the easy-listening tradition of pop music as much as against war and American society.

Miles Davis's 1960 album *Kind of Blue* is a reminder that modern jazz was, for many people, the in sound at the start of the decade.

For a culture shock, it is worth listening to one of the popular '60s musicians most people can't stand any longer—for example, the Incredible String Band or Leonard Cohen. Raid your parents' or grandparents' record collection. It is good to get a feel of the original albums in their 1960s record sleeves and to hear them on a turntable.

Art and architecture

Most modern art collections have paintings by '60s artists such as Warhol, Lichtenstein, and Hockney, and works by Claes Oldenburg, Anthony Caro, and other sculptors of the period.

Sixties architecture is visible in most cities, especially in the form of run-down housing developments.

Quotations

The quotations in this book are from the following sources:

Page 5:   Dotson Rader, *Tennessee Williams: Cry of the Heart*, New York: Doubleday, 1988

Page 8:   Ronald Fraser, *1968, A Student Generation in Revolt*, Chatto and Windus, 1988

Page 14:   Marshall McLuhan, *The Gutenberg Galaxy*, 1968

Page 17:   Rachel Carson, *Silent Spring*, 1962

Page 18:   *Harper's and Queen* magazine, May 1973

Page 25:   Jonathon Green, *Days in the Life*, Heinemann-Mandarin, 1988

Page 27:   Jonathon Green, *Days in the Life*, Heinemann-Mandarin, 1988

Page 28:   Ian Chilvers, Harold Osborne, Dennis Farr, *The Oxford Dictionary of Art*, Oxford University Press, 1988

Page 31:   Jonathon Green, *Days in the Life*, Heinemann-Mandarin, 1988

Page 34:   Jack Nicklaus with Ken Bowden, *My Story*, New York: Simon & Schuster, 1997

Page 37:   Robert Andrews, *Dictionary of Contemporary Quotations*, Cassell, 1997

Page 41:   as told to the author.

Index